OLD STIRLING

Elspeth King

Livestock being driven down Wallace Street, c.1910.

ISBN 9781840334517

A view of Barnton Street by A.D.S MacPherson, c.1965.

Acknowledgements

The poem 'Stirling' by Arthur Johnston (c.1579–1641), translated by Professor Robert Crawford, is from the book *Apollos of the North – Selected Poems of George Buchanan and Arthur Johnston*, edited by Robert Crawford, published by Polygon (2006; ISBN 10: 1 90459881 1), an imprint of Birlinn Ltd. It is used with the kind permission of the editor and publisher.

Most of the photographs in this book are from the collections of the Stirling Smith Art Gallery and Museum, with others from the collection of Richard Stenlake, and remain within their copyright (or that of the original photographer). The photograph on page 10 belongs to Malcolm Allan.

The author would like to thank the people who have donated photographs to the collections of the Stirling Smith Art Gallery and Museum over the past 130 years, and the many individuals who have helped with information and advice. J. Malcolm Allan, W.F.T. Anderson, Wilson Asher, Anne Ballantyne, Alex Bean, Alex Black, Pamela Brown, Caroline Buchanan, Evelyn and John Cameron, Central Scotland Police, George Dixon, Michael Donnelly, Betty Duncan, Lesley Duncan, Ken Dunn, Dorothy Hayes, Eric Hamilton, Margaret Job, Mike Jodeluk, Gary Lawrie, Elma Lindsay, Willie More, Dr Ken Mackay, Robert McEwen, Dr Rennie and Agnes McOwan, John Murphy, Peter Paterson, Marion Peat, John Ramsay, Frank Saunders, Mrs M. Sinclair, Mrs M. Watson, Eunice and Ian Wyles, J.M. Young, and the late Bob McCutcheon are among those who helped with information. Text management was by Thomas Christie. The advice and patience of editor David Pettigrew of Stenlake Publishing Ltd has been much appreciated.

The Stirling Smith photographic collection has been curated by Michael McGinnes for the past thirty years and, as he has been responsible for digitisation and computerisation, this book is largely his. All textual errors belong to the author, who is still trying to comprehend and interpret the richness, beauty and many-layered history of Stirling.

Introduction

Who can do Stirling justice? Cradle of kings
Who set their castle strong on its high ridge
Its fresh air keeps that great outpost of heaven
Secure there, safe from enemy attack
Towering on its matched rocks, its own towers match
The towers of Jove by Rome's Tarpeian Rock
Nobly the River Forth lets itself flow
Underneath two fine triumphal arches
Hesitantly, often turning back,
Winding like Phrygia's River Maeander
It moves with a light touch and takes it time
The town and country smile, gifted with riches
But Stirling's fame in war is even more
Worth epic celebration. More than once
This place repelled the spears of Rome, its river
Commanded Rome's imperial eagle, *Stop*!
    Arthur Johnston (1579–1641)
    Translated from the Latin by Robert Crawford

Stirling is a place of enduring and iconic beauty. Writers have vied with each other to extol the beauty of the landscape and the splendours of the scenic views. Artists have come to Stirling to paint these views or find inspiration in them. Sculptors have embellished the cityscape with figures from Stirling's stirring past.

In many ways the heart of Scotland, Stirling has always been at the crossroads of the country's geography and history. It has been described as 'the brooch which clasps the Highlands and Lowlands together'. In mediaeval times it was certainly a frontier town and the first visitors were invaders. The beast of Stirling, which is shared with Rome, is the wolf. According to legend, when Stirling was under attack from Viking invaders, a wolf howled, alerting the townspeople in time to save the town. The earliest representation of the Stirling Wolf is on the Stirling Jug of 1457, one of the standard Scottish liquid measures. The wolf can also be seen represented on many buildings throughout the town.

The seal of Stirling, which dates from 1296, exemplifies this frontier nature, with the Castle on one side and the bridge over the Forth, with its armies, on the other. The Latin inscription translates as 'In this is contained the Castle and Bridge of Stirling. Here stand the Scots, supported by the Cross; here stand the Bruti, supported by their arms'. The crucifix on the centre of the bridge either represents a shrine or a chapel. In the middle ages, Scotland was believed to be almost completely surrounded by water (the marshy waters of the Forth and the Clyde were thought to be 'the sea of

Scotland'), connected to the rest of Britain only by the bridge of Stirling. With peat clearance, drainage and land management, the countryside changed considerably in the eighteenth century, but before then every invader coming to Scotland aimed for the bridge and it was said, 'to take Stirling is to hold Scotland'. The Castle was there to protect that important crossing point. The images and the inscription on the seal are thought to mean that while armies may come to Stirling with all their might, the Scots have God on their side. The idea is memorialised in verse:

    The Britons stand by force of arms
    The Scots are by this cross preserved from harms
    The castle and bridge of Stirling town
    Are in the compass of this seal set down.

Six battles, which changed the course of Scottish history, took place in and around Stirling, the most famous of which were Stirling Bridge (11 September 1297) and Bannockburn (23/24 June 1314), the victories of Wallace and Bruce respectively against English armies.

The Stewart kings, descendants of Robert Bruce's daughter Margery, had Stirling as their favoured residence and so for centuries it might be said that the history of Stirling was the history of Scotland. The town became one of the original four Royal Burghs of Scotland in the 1120s, with charters from King Alexander I granting trading privileges to facilitate better service to the royal court in the Castle. The Seven Incorporated Trades of the mediaeval burgh were certainly service trades such as hammermen, weavers, tailors, shoemakers, butchers, skinners and bakers.

The burgh lost much status and sense of purpose when the royal court moved south in 1603, after the Union of the Crowns, but Stirling was still of great strategic importance and the Castle became a significant base for the army. From the eighteenth to the mid-twentieth century, Stirling was very much a garrison town. This resulted in the disintegration of the fabric of the Stewart court in Stirling Castle, with the Chapel Royal, Great Hall and Palace used for barracks and ordnance. When one of the carved Stirling Heads, a series of ancient oak effigies carved in the Palace, came loose from the ceiling of the King's Chambers in 1777, the rest were dismantled and discarded. Wainscot panelling and paintings were also removed and, even in the present century, items 'thrown out of Stirling Castle' still appear in national auction houses. When Robert Burns visited Stirling in August 1787, he was dismayed by the condition of Stirling and its Castle and etched his 'Stirling

The Stirling Jug.

Lines' in response on a window pane of Wingate's Inn, now the Golden Lion Hotel.

The perceived threat of French invasion led to an increase in the provision for the army in the period 1790–1820; later on, in 1886, the government bought the Forthside estate to house the ordnance depot. A large tract of the riverside became a military zone, which was extended by two world wars. Until the eighteenth century, Stirling Harbour had hosted ships from the Netherlands, Scandinavia and the Baltic, but the First World War saw the closure of the river to even pleasure traffic. During the Second World War, the Royal Army Ordnance Corps headquarters for Scotland were at Forthside, Stirling. Many of the regiments raised for both world wars were kitted, trained and processed through Stirling, and a large number of civilian buildings were requisitioned for military purposes.

Although Stirling was a base for the military, it was also a market town and the county town. The County Club, and the Annual County Ball, were important institutions for most of the nineteenth and twentieth centuries. Because of the historic architectural infrastructure of the Castle, Church of the Holy Rude, the Tolbooth, Cowane's Hospital where the Guildry met, and the Sheriff Court, traditions were carried on in Stirling when they had been quietly dropped in other places. When the Circuit Court came to Stirling the hospitality provided by the Provost, magistrates and Castle Governor for the visiting judges, turned into a major social occasion. The Kirking o' the Council still takes place, after a local authority election, in the Church of the Holy Rude. Stirling burgh officers were first clad in red in 1607. In the eighteenth century, the uniform consisted of a red jacket and knee breeches, white stockings and a tricorn hat. The council officers or halberdiers were also given a sword and halberd to protect the Provost. Distinctive uniforms of this style were still being worn in 1952 when the accession of Queen Elizabeth was proclaimed by the Provost and magistrates at the Mercat Cross in Broad Street. The Guildry of Stirling still meets in Cowane's Hospital today.

Scales of Justice from Stirling Tolbooth.

Stirling was also the nodal point where the drove roads of Scotland converged, from the Highlands and Islands, bringing the traditional black Highland cattle to the October trysts for onward sale to Falkirk, Carlisle and Smithfield. The cattle trade gave rise to the brief appearance of Scotland's only school of animal art, run in Stirling by Joseph Denovan Adam (1841–1896). Although the locations of the cattle markets have changed, Stirling still retains two marts in the twenty-first century.

On account of the beauty of the landscape, Stirling was on the itinerary of every landscape painter of note. The earliest surviving landscape was painted by the Dutch artist Johannes Vostermann (1643–1699), court painter to Charles II. The English artist Joseph Farington (1747–1821) thought that Stirling had few rivals for beauty, and he was given the Freedom of the Burgh in 1788 for his artistic work. Other visiting painters included Alexander Nasmyth, Thomas Hofland, Thomas Fenwick, Horatio MacCulloch, Thomas Hearne, Edward Dayes, Francis Nicholson, Henry Brocas, John Varley, Copley Fielding, John Glover, Samuel Prout, J.D. Harding, George Fennel Robertson and William Turner. In the period 1890–1920, many of the so-called Glasgow Boys (William Kennedy, James Guthrie, Crawford Shaw, George Henry and A.E. Hornel) spent their summers in Stirling and Cambuskenneth.

For the same reason, there has always been a tourist trade in Stirling. The development of modern tourism in the area took place after the publication in 1810 of Sir Walter Scott's *Lady of the Lake* (which is set in Stirling and the Trossachs), the advent of steamer traffic on the River Forth, and the introduction of the railway in 1848.

By the early twentieth century, Stirling had developed a great sense of its own identity and of its importance both in Scotland's history and current affairs. In 1905, the Member of Parliament was Sir Henry Campbell-Bannerman, who was also the Liberal leader and Prime Minister. Naturally, the parliamentary constituency of Stirling Burghs was the focus of attention at that time and when Campbell-Bannerman died in 1908, every woman's suffrage organisation came to Stirling for the by-election, an occasion which gave a great boost to the cause of women's suffrage in Scotland. The political and social emancipation of women is one of the recurrent themes of twentieth century history. Although the Scottish fight was begun in Stirling, it took until 1975 before Stirling got its first woman Provost (Laura McCabe), and until 1997 before Anne McGuire became the town's first woman MP.

Nevertheless, Stirling has always remained a place of political significance. In 1928, a young boy on holiday in the town was standing beside Campbell-Bannerman's statue at the Corn Exchange, listening to his father discussing Campbell-Bannerman's impact on British politics. At this point, the boy decided he might go into politics himself and run the country like Campbell-Bannerman. His name was Harold Wilson, twice Prime Minister.

Also, in 1928 the National Party of Scotland was established in Stirling by Robert Bontine Cunninghame Graham, the aristocratic laird of Gartmore and novelist, horseman and radical politician. This later became the Scottish National Party and the first SNP Member of Parliament was the consultant chest physician at Stirling Royal Infirmary, Dr Robert McIntyre, who was elected in 1945 for the Motherwell constituency. Dr McIntyre became a town councillor in Stirling in 1956 and Provost in 1967. For a generation, he was the public face of the SNP, serving as Chairman (1948–1958) and as President (1958–1980).

Between 1983 and 1997 Michael Forsyth was MP for Stirling, and also held the position of Secretary of State for Scotland, ensuring that significant sums of money were spent on re-shaping Stirling Castle into a major tourist destination. The story of Stirling in the last forty years is that of the retreat of the army, which moved out of the Castle in 1964. This will be complete when the former military area of Forthside is again available as public space.

Stirling has always possessed and understood the concept of historical continuity. For the first 34 years of the twentieth century, the burgh was essentially run by two men – David Buchan Morris, the Town Clerk, and Andrew H. Goudie, the Burgh Surveyor. In 1934, both of them received the Freedom of the Burgh of Stirling, in a joint ceremony. David Morris, who was also an historian, gave an account of all those who had received the Freedom of Stirling since mediaeval times, and explained in detail what it meant when free men swore to bear scot and lot and to do watch and ward for the Royal Burgh. Both men also reflected on the enormous changes which had taken place in their time – the advent of the motor car, the need to reshape the roads in and out of Stirling (for these were the roads which served all of the traffic travelling from north to south in Scotland), the need to secure a decent water supply, and to provide municipal housing for the working population of the factories, mines and engineering shops of Stirling. They reckoned that the introduction of asphalt on the roads after the Great War was the single most important factor in improving the quality of life, and ridding the streets of noise and dirt. The Limner and Trinidad Asphalt company even set up a depot in the burgh.

Morris and Goudie had served under seven Provosts and each was pretty powerful in his own sphere. Morris ran the

Scottish Convention of Royal Burghs and Goudie was President of the Institute of Water Engineers. They ran a tight ship in Stirling.

The town was exceptionally well run, and it did not have the huge social problems faced by other Scottish cities. In that same year of 1934, Lewis Grassic Gibbon and Hugh MacDiarmid published an important book, *The Scottish Scene*, which looked at those problems. Grassic Gibbon had a colourful turn of phrase and personified the Scottish cities as women. Edinburgh was a disappointed spinster, with a harelip and inhibitions. Dundee was a frowsy fisher wife, addicted to gin and infanticide. Aberdeen was a thin-lipped peasant woman who had borne eleven children and buried nine. Glasgow, the vomit of a cataleptic commercialism, a corpse on which the maggot-swarm was fiercely alive, was likened to the Hindu goddess Siva, the Destroyer, with her waistlet of skulls.

Grassic Gibbon and MacDiarmid did not mention Stirling in their book. MacDiarmid in particular would say nothing derogatory about Stirling, the home of the great Scottish publisher Eneas Mackay, who published so much important Scottish poetry, including MacDiarmid's own. Stirling was home to two major publishing houses in the twentieth century (the other was the Drummond Tract Depot), and every writer had cause to be grateful for that.

The sense of historical continuity in Stirling is powerful. In the twentieth century, in 1967, the University was brought into being. In the sixteenth century, Stirling was home to George Buchanan, one of the greatest scholars and teachers in Europe, and his pupil, the young King James VI. In 1911 flight was pioneered in Stirling by the Barnwell Brothers. Yet it was in 1507 that the first Stirling flight pioneer, the friar John Damien, tried to fly from the castle walls with a pair of wings. There is nothing new under the sun. In 2002, Stirling became Scotland's newest city, but people had always believed it to be a city. The inscription on John Cowane's charter chest of 1636 reads 'John Cowanes gift to ye citie of Sterling'.

Stirling is home to the world's oldest curling stone and football.

5

The Stirling Smith Art Gallery and Museum is the repository for John Cowane's charter chest and many other key objects from Stirling's past. As it is the source for many of the photographs in this book, it is also the starting point for the journey through the images of old Stirling. Many people begin their local history research projects at the Smith. Others contribute to the collection by donation, or by lending their photographs for copying. Some forty local groups, from the Astronomical Society to the Sugarcraft Guild, meet here in the evenings to pursue their common interests. A programme of changing exhibitions and the Stirling Story presentation ensures that the building is always busy with visitors.

The Stirling Smith was established as the Smith Institute through the bequest of the artist Thomas Stuart Smith (1815–1869) (*right*) and first opened to the public on 11 August 1874 (the name changed about a century later). Smith, trained in Italy, was 'a man who could paint anything' according to one of his pupils, and was highly regarded by contemporary artists. Sir Edwin Landseer and John Phillip R.A. were among his admirers. Smith bequeathed all of his own paintings and those in his collection, together with a sum of money to build and maintain an institute for the inhabitants of Stirling, Dunblane and Kinbuck, provided that the burgh of Stirling supplied a suitable plot of land. Smith had intended to supervise the building programme himself, but he died within a month of signing his will, and two years before the selection of the site. The building was designed by Edinburgh architect John Lessels (1808–1883), whose son James was involved in the design of the Public Library in Corn Exchange Road in 1903.

Alexander Croall (1804–1885), first curator of the Smith Institute, was a native of Angus who became nationally known as a natural historian. He was also the first curator of Derby City Museum before his appointment to Stirling. He corresponded with, and was respected by, other eminent natural historians, including Balfour, Dickie, Hooker and Darwin. Sir William Hooker commissioned him to prepare a herbarium of the plants of Braemar for Queen Victoria.

Croall is still remembered for his standard four-volume work *British Sea Weeds: Nature Printed*, published in 1860. His passion for seaweed gave rise to his nickname 'Roosty Tangle'. Croall's professionalism was praised by the eminent author Samuel Smiles who noted that under his curatorship, the Smith Institute became one of the best provincial museums in Britain. Croall's curatorship lasted twelve years, until his death.

The main picture gallery of the Smith Institute in the late nineteenth century. Measuring 30.7m by 12.9m and with a height of 6.09m, it is still the biggest exhibition space in central Scotland. It was designed to exhibit the Smith's collection of oil paintings, currently 1,000 in number, which date from the seventeenth century to the present day.

Until the building of the Albert Halls in 1883, this was also the main concert hall for Stirling. The Smith trustees insisted on the creation of a purpose-built concert hall, fearing that the paintings would be damaged. Nevertheless, large concerts were still held in the years before the outbreak of the Second World War as part of the events programme of the triennial Stirling Fine Arts Association Exhibitions.

Since the year 2000, this area has been occupied with the Stirling Story presentation, which charts Stirling's history from prehistoric times to the present.

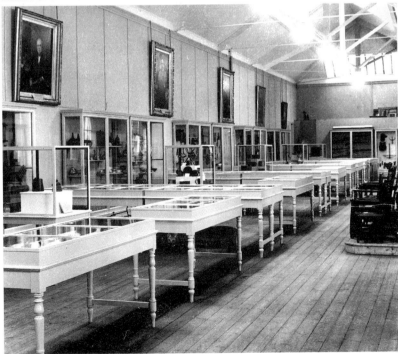

The museum gallery of the Smith Institute, c.1930. From the beginning, the Smith's curators built up an important collection covering many aspects of the material culture of both Scottish and local history. Star objects include the Stirling Jug (the Scots Pint measure, instituted by Act of Parliament in 1457), the oldest curling stone in the world (1511), the oldest football in the world (c.1540) and a figure of Justice from the Stirling Tolbooth which is so old that she does not have a blindfold. Loans were made regularly to major exhibitions, including the Glasgow International Exhibitions of 1888 and 1901, the Scottish National History Exhibition of 1911, and the Empire Exhibition of 1938. The Stirling Smith continues to build new collections, add to the existing ones, and lend to other museums and galleries on a regular basis. As museums now co-operate internationally, loans have been made to Amsterdam, Hamburg and New York in recent years. The old museum gallery is currently a storage area for the Smith's growing collections.

James Sword was the second curator of the Smith Institute, from 1885 until 1921. This photograph of him, with his gun dog Bob, was taken in the grounds of the Smith in 1914. Sword was a keen natural historian and sportsman with skills in taxidermy. He created a large collection of stuffed birds and animals, and put together the collection of communion tokens. He also did much to improve the grounds, making pavements, concrete kerbings and bases for the iron railings round the building.

The Smith Institute was designed with accommodation for the curator. The first three curators lived there, and in the early years, kept sheep on the two acres of ground surrounding the building. During the military use of the building, the curators remained on site to care for the collections and the building. A caretaker was resident until 1970. In the 1980s, the residential area was developed for office and public use.

In 2002, the grounds of the Smith were developed by the Friends of the Smith as a biodiversity area for teaching natural history and environmental issues, literally 'grounds for learning', and as an alternative to the way in which these subjects were previously taught, using stuffed animals.

Many civic events have taken place at the Smith. This is a gathering of the Incorporated Glasgow Stirlingshire and Sons of the Rock Society. The Glasgow Stirlingshire Society was originally established in 1809 to help Stirling people who found themselves in difficult circumstances in industrial Glasgow. The Sons of the Rock are a local charity – anyone born within sight of Stirling Castle is a Son of the Rock – and the two combined in 1870 with the express purpose of raising money and celebrating Auld Hansel Monday.

In Scotland gifts were traditionally given at New Year rather than Christmas, on Auld Hansel Monday, the 'visiting day'. In 1752 the European calendar was changed and eleven days were cut from it to bring the seasons back into line. When the New Year came round, there were widespread protests at the 'eleven lost days' and most Scots insisted that Hansel Monday could only take place on the first Monday after the eleven lost days were counted – the first Monday after the twelfth of January. Auld Hansel Monday was maintained as a holiday in most Scottish towns for well over 100 years, until people forgot the reason for it. Stirling is almost the last place in Scotland where the celebration is maintained. The Sons of the Rock levy a fine on members who cannot attend the Auld Hansel Monday event, and the funds of this ancient charity are replenished and disbursed each year. Note the Burgh Officer in his traditional red uniform and cocked hat, standing on the sculpture plinth on the left.

Although, with the lines of machinists, this photograph looks like it was taken in a clothing factory or sweatshop, the location is in fact the main picture gallery of the Smith Institute in 1919. In 1914, the Smith Institute was requisitioned for military purposes by the War Department, along with most other public buildings in Stirling. The collection had to be crammed into the smaller rooms as the larger spaces were used as barracks. By 1919, the Smith was being used as a machining factory for army uniforms. One of the machinists in the photograph, Mrs Joanne Jack, lost her husband in the Great War. He never knew his daughter. The Smith did not become a museum and gallery again until 1921. The experience was repeated again from 1939 to 1947, with bad results for the building and its collections.

The reopening ceremony of the Smith Institute in 1948. The reopening was performed by Dr T.J. Honeyman (standing on the platform), the art dealer and later director of Kelvingrove Art Gallery. Seated at the table is Alastair McMichael, Provost of Stirling (1945–1949) and to the right of him is Dr Robert McIntyre (1913–1998) of Stirling Royal Infirmary, and a Smith Trustee. Dr McIntyre was later Provost of Stirling from 1967 to 1975. The ceremony took place in the Smith's largest gallery, with most of the permanent collection on the walls. Notable is the large painting directly behind the table; this is the work of Archibald Russell Watson Allan RSA (1878–1959), commissioned for the 1935 Stirling Fine Art Association exhibition. It was later purchased and presented to the Smith and is a striking artistic celebration of horsepower, which in the 1930s was being phased out in favour of the tractor. The artist was a Stirling resident and, as his studio at his home in Randolph Road could not accommodate paintings of this size, it was actually painted in the Smith.

Museum Hall, Bridge of Allan (centre foreground), was built in 1886 as the successor to the three-storey Macfarlane Natural History Museum of 1860 (left background). Both were funded through the generosity of John Macfarlane of Coneyhill (1785–1868) who made his fortune in textiles in Manchester, and who spent it introducing the principle of free libraries and museums in his native Stirling. He opened the town's first free library and his Natural History Museum contained a major collection of stuffed animals and birds from all over the world, sourced at a time when taxidermy was the main way of studying exotic creatures. It also had a fine collection of plaster casts of Classical statues. The first museum was demolished in 1905, and the Museum Hall collection fell victim to the requisitioning of two World Wars when it was used for target practice. Some of the Macfarlane collection of antiquities was moved to the Smith when Museum Hall was built in 1886, as it functioned mainly as a concert hall for Bridge of Allan and Stirling.

Museum Hall was designed by Stirling architect Ebenezer Simpson (1854–1934) and, for over a century, was recognised worldwide as an excellent concert hall. It is now (2009) in the process of conversion to housing.

COLLECTION

OF

INTERESTING OBJECTS IN THIS (McFarlane) MUSEUM.

transferred to Smith

Chair of Rev. James Guthrie, Minister of the First Charge, Stirling, who suffered martyrdom at Edinburgh, 1st June, 1661.

Two Chairs from the Castle, beautifully carved.

A Chair which belonged to Donaldson, the "King o' the Muirs," on which James V. sat, when having been benighted out hunting, and separated from his attendants, he happened to enter a cottage in a muir at the foot of the Ochils, near Alloa, where he was kindly received.

Two Curling Stones of extremely primitive formation, one inscribed "St. Js. B. Stirling, 1511," one of the oldest in Scotland, the other being evidently still older. There are indentations on the upper and lower surfaces for convenience in grasping. Curling, it may be stated, is first mentioned as a Scottish game about the year 1410.

Two upper stones of Querns or hand-mills, used for grinding corn, prior to the introduction of grinding by water. In 1284, it was statute that "na man sall presume to grind quheit, maishlock or rye, wit hand-mylnes except he be compelit be storm, or be lack o' mylnes quilk sall grind the samin, and in this cas., gif a man grinds at hand-mylnes, he sall git thirteen measures off as multure, and gif anie man contravenis this our prohibition, he sall tyne his hand-mylnes perpetualie." The Quern was to be found in use in remote districts up to the end of last century.

Two Canoes, one from the Chinese seas, deposited by Sir James Alexander, length 12 feet 10 inches.

Portrait of Rev. James Guthrie.

One of the original oak carvings, from the ceiling of the Presence Chamber of Stirling Castle. These carvings, as appears from the record of the Lord High Treasurer, were executed by John Drummond of Auchterarder, Master of Works to James V., a cadet of the noble house of Perth.

Four Canoe Models.

Twenty porphyry cannon balls from Fort-William, recently presented by Mr Ainslie, Fort-William.

Iron gad, with which those under sentence of death in Stirling were secured.

Mask and hatchet used by the executioner in decapitating Baird and Hardie at Stirling.

Cap which was worn by Burke the murderer, and which was presented to a person in Stirling by Mr Christie, keeper of the Edinburgh prison.

The jegg or jougs formerly attached to the market cross of Stirling. The criminal had his neck and wrists enclosed in this instrument for a certain period daily during the term of his imprisonment.

Three spear heads, found on the top of the Abbey Craig, along with a stone bearing the inscription, "The Cross of Peace."

Nepaul firelock and sword gun.

Bayonets from Inkermann and the Redan.

Skull or cranium of an animal, probably the wolf, found imbedded in blue clay, 20 feet under the surface, when the workmen were preparing the foundation of the New Bridge of Stirling.

Part of the original cornice of the Douglas Room in the Castle.

An ancient time-piece.

Large painting of the arms of the town of Stirling, supposed to have been painted on the occasion of the visit of Charles II. to the burgh.

Old allegorical painting, the property of the burgh.

Original sketch, by Alfred Crowquill, of London.

Petrified wood from Tasmania.

Part of the skin of a rhinoceros.

Books on theology and ecclesiastical history which belonged to James Guthrie, Minister of Stirling.

An excellent collection of minerals of the district arranged in glass cases. Among these are some very interesting fossils.

Horse shoe, found in Milton bog on the field of Bannockburn.

Ancient Celt or Stone Hatchet, found ten feet under the surface in Blairdrummond Moss.

Part of the pulpit in which Knox preached a the coronation of James VI. in the West Church of Stirling, on the 29th July, 1567.

Charred wheat, found at the Roman Camp, Castlecarry.

Calthrop found when draining the field of Bannockburn.

A Collection of British and Continental coins in silver and copper, including silver coins of Edward I. and Queen Elizabeth, and copper coins of James I. of Scotland.

Casts of various Scottish burgh and other seals.

A five shilling bank-note of the B k of Stirling.

Chinese illuminated M , and other Chinese ornaments.

Japanese smoking pipe.

Various Chinese ornaments, idols, &c.

Piece of Otaheite cloth, made from the bark of trees.

Part of skeleton of whale found at Airthrey, 1819.

Part of vertebræ of whale found at Stirling, 1857.

An interesting collection of stuffed animals.

Hangman's Cap for measuring the Stirling burgh executioner's allowance of grain.

Douglas Room, Stirling Castle.

Another important collection of antiquities in Stirling was held in the Douglas Room in Stirling Castle. This room is now within the part of the Castle given over to the Museum of the Argyll and Sutherland Highlanders. It was so named because it was the place where King James II stabbed the eighth Earl of Douglas in 1452, before throwing his body from the window. The ground below is still known as the Douglas Gardens.

This part of the Castle has been altered many times and in the early nineteenth century the room was part of the complex which was the home of the Governor of Stirling Castle. It was later used for general army purposes, and was partly destroyed in a fire in 1855. This photograph from the 1890s (*upper left*) was taken during the room's time as a small museum, developed for Stirling's then nascent tourist industry (hundreds of Mauchline Ware souvenirs, inscribed 'sold in the Douglas Room', are in private collections today). According to *Shearer's Guide Book*, published around that time, it contained 'the Communion Table used in the Castle by John Knox; the old pulpit from the Chapel Royal called Knox's Pulpit; oak model of the old Scottish crown; old timepiece from the reign of James V, from Linlithgow Palace; chair of James VI; old chair from the reign of James II; Lochaber Axe found on the Field of Bannockburn; the Tilting Lance of James VI; pikes used at the Radical Rising at Bonnymuir'. Nothing of this has survived and, even in the present century, paintings and antiquities 'discarded from Stirling Castle' still appear in auction houses.

The Douglas Window is above the arch on the left. The main elevation on the right was rebuilt in the Baronial style by the architect Robert Billings after the 1855 fire. Known as the King's Old Building, this part of the Castle is now the home of the Museum of the Argyll and Sutherland Highlanders.

Raploch Quarry was opened in the eighteenth century. Situated at the foot of the Castle Rock on the north-west side, it was the source of the fine sandstone from which the Stirling Smith and many other Victorian buildings in the King's Park, Bridge of Allan and Dunblane areas were built.

The Quarry later flooded (see opposite) and was then filled in with Stirling's refuse in the early 1940s. In 1965, the present Stirling Fire Station was built there and accommodates the official helicopter landing pad for the area. This is often used by royal visitors and, on occasion, for transferring mountain rescue casualties to Stirling Royal Infirmary.

The Concise Scots Dictionary (Aberdeen University Press, 1985) defines the word *Raploch* as 'grey, coarse, homespun, undyed, woollen cloth, or a garment made from this'. In the sixteenth century, *Raploch* was the word used to describe the everyday clothing of the Scottish people; the 'unmaist claith of Raploch gray' was the grey woollen overcoat of the Poor Man in Sir David Lindsay's play *The Satire of the Three Estates* (1540), and such a garment was commonly forfeited to the Church as part of death duties if money or animals were not available. However, generally speaking, the adjective was used to denote something ordinary, undistinguished, but necessary, honest and serviceable. Thus, Raploch was the service area for Stirling Castle. In the time of King James IV, the royal washerwomen lived there.

Below: In the early years of the twentieth century, the former Raploch Quarry area flooded, providing a picturesque view favoured by many producers of postcards. The small farming settlement at the foot of Ballengeich Road, shown here, is part of Raploch village as listed in the *Ordnance Gazetteer of Scotland* (1893).

The Ballengeich Road is the steep roadway which winds down the north side of the Castle Rock, providing a secondary exit from Stirling Castle. King James V was popularly known as 'the Gude Man [i.e. farmer] of Ballengeich' as he had the habit of going out of the Castle, in disguise, to mix with ordinary people and there are many tales of his escapades. A chair he sat on when visiting a local farmhouse while posing as the 'Gude Man' is in the Smith collections. When the farmer later found out the identity of his guest, he kept the chair.

Apart from being the Castle back door and service area, Raploch was also a weaving village and fishing settlement. Indeed, the first planned housing scheme, Fisher's Row, was established there in 1693 by Stirling Burgh to give encouragement to the fishing industry on the Forth.

After it was filled with household refuse, it became the Quarry Park and was for many years used as a track for harness racing, a sport favoured by the Romany community, who often camped in this area. After Stirling Fire Station was built on the site, the trotting track moved to Corbiewood, near Bannockburn, where it flourishes still.

Travelling people and gypsies were associated with the Raploch area, where many spent the winter. Their bright caravans were an attraction to local children in the 1950s. This camp was photographed at least 50 years earlier and was the type of picturesque scene which attracted the artists now known as the Glasgow Boys. Tom Austen Brown's major work, *The Gypsy Camp* (now in Glasgow's Kelvingrove Art Gallery and Museum) was painted during his stay in the artist's colony of Cambuskenneth.

Raploch Road, *c*.1900, looking from north to south, with the Castle visible on the left. Note the lack of road surface at this time. Housing was built only on the east side; the west side was farmland. In his *Old Faces, Old Places, Old Stories of Stirling* (two volumes, 1896–1899), William Drysdale refers to Raploch being a pretty place when it was weaving village, with flower beds in front of the houses and well-kept gardens to the rear of the houses. It subsequently became a colony of Irish immigrant workers.

Raploch Road, looking from south to north, *c*.1900.

Farm workers in Raploch. From the mid-eighteenth century, the agricultural improvements which created the farmland on the Carse of Stirling gave rise to the need for seasonal labour for ploughing, planting and harvesting. The stripping of oak bark for tanning was another seasonal occupation. In the mid-nineteenth century the Potato Famine in Ireland forced many people to emigrate in search of work, and Raploch at one time was known as 'Little Ireland'.

Harvesting oats with a three-horse Massey-Harris binder (manufactured in Toronto) on a field on Kings Park Farm, at the foot of Stirling Castle, in the decade 1925–1935. The photographer was positioned at the dyke on the former Clay Toll Brae. The King's Knott, the renaissance remnant of the royal gardens in Kings Park, still survives in the area to the right of this scene. In the left background the houses are those of the Ballengeich Road, beyond which is Raploch.

Tattie howkers, 1940, from the collection of James Gray and Co., Seed and Agricultural Merchants. Gray's, established in Stirling in 1865, were one of the main seed merchants in Scotland. They operated internationally for a time but ceased trading in April 1984. The location of the photograph is unknown.

Raploch residents, at the foot of the area known as 'Minister's Row'. The woman on the far right was called Nappy Coan.

Mrs Ging, with her donkey and cart, outside the Albert Hall, Dumbarton Road. Mrs Ging was a hawker of rags and second-hand goods, and lived at the Top of the Town before moving to Raploch. She also kept pigs at home, and children could take the family brock pail (of potato peelings and vegetable waste) for pig feed in exchange for Mrs Ging's homemade toffee – a 1930s example of waste recycling! Stirling was the market town for the large farming county, and the keeping of pigs and chickens by urban dwellers was common until after the Second World War.

Raploch Farm, Drip Road, 1927. The farm was worked from 1927 to 1936 by Robert L. Ballantyne of the Barnton Dairy on Stirling's Barnton Street. He came from a dairying family in Glasgow, and obtained the tenancy from Cowane's Trust. This fine photograph was taken by Charles Reid of Wishaw to show off the farm building and the herd of Ayrshire dairy cattle. This was the first herd in Stirlingshire to be tuberculin-tested.

Raploch was very much a rural community at this time; further along the road was the Stirling Combination Hospital (now Kildean Hospital), built in 1903/04 so that those with infectious diseases could be isolated. However, St Mark's Church of Scotland was built on the site of the farm in 1964 to serve the post-war Raploch housing scheme.

This is Mary Anderson, who was one of the first people to be moved from the old housing at the Top of the Town to the new municipal housing in Raploch in 1928. She was aged six when her family moved and remained a resident there for the rest of her life. On leaving school, she trained as a milk tester and drove around the local farms, taking milk samples for testing at a depot in Port Street. She drove ambulances during the Second World War.

The Stirling Ceresan Mixer by Robertson and McLaren. Ceresan was a dressing used for oats and grain prior to sowing. The dressing stopped vermin from eating the grain as Ceresan was a poisonous substance and farm workers often used masks when handling it. It was popular in the inter-war years. Robertson and McLaren were a Stirling-based company supplying farmers' requisites.

In an agricultural community, dealing with grain-raiding vermin was always a major consideration. Immediately after the Second World War, there was a full-time rat catcher on the staff of the Sanitary Inspector's department. He had the task of surveying farms, grain stores, hotels, restaurants and shops and giving advice on how to keep the premises vermin-free.

Duncan's Lemonade Factory, Drip Road, Raploch. This small factory had its origins in a brewery in Broad Street at the Top of the Town. The Raploch site was a processing plant attached to an old farmhouse. Production of Duncan's Soft Drinks lasted for three generations from around 1900 until 1992.

Duncan's Lemonade was popular as a mixer drink, particularly for whisky, within central Scotland. Pure citrus extract was used in the manufacture, which ensured that the lemonade did not have an overtly sweet taste. Many people would not drink whisky without Duncan's Lemonade.

Duncan's fleet of six lorries was the pride of Raploch. They were immaculately kept and had beautifully painted rear boards featuring Old Stirling Bridge and the Wallace Monument. The plant on Drip Road, where the lorries were also garaged, was situated near the bridge. The name Drip Road refers to the Drip Moss, which was drained in the eighteenth century. Formerly a main entry route into Stirling, it now serves the Raploch area alone.

Duncan's was one of the last firms in Stirling to use horse-drawn vehicles. Pictured here in the mid 1950s, Jock was the last horse and he was looked after by Jimmy Wright, who apparently 'looked after' all the women in Stirling too! The 1950s council housing on the north side of Drip Road can be seen in the background.

Hamish Duncan, Managing Director, in Duncan's factory yard on the day of his retiral in 1987. The firm was sold to Joseph Dunn of Glasgow. Duncan's employed a workforce of 32 people, mostly resident in Raploch, when it finally closed in 1992.

Asher's Ice Cream was founded by William Asher (1900–1952) in 1933. He erected the first purpose-built ice cream factory in Scotland on the north side of Drip Road in 1948. With dairy farming in the vicinity, the factory was ideally situated and, like Duncan's on the opposite side of the street, it is a family business, delivering its product within a 30-mile radius of Stirling. The business is still in operation and continues to maintain a fleet of vans.

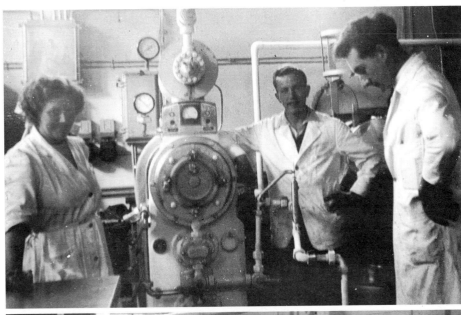

The interior of Asher's ice cream factory, *c*.1950. Throughout its history, the business has won many awards for its product, which is highly prized in Stirlingshire. Although Asher's stopped making ice cream in Raploch in 2006, the product is made to their recipe elsewhere and then packaged and distributed from Raploch plant.

A group of workers at W. Alexander & Sons Ltd Coach Building Works on Drip Road, 1939. Coach trimmer Bill McNab is the young man sitting on the bench, centre front.

The business started as a cycle-building shop in Camelon in 1902 and this extensive coach-building works was opened in Raploch in 1931, building mainly single-decker buses. When it outgrew the site, the works were moved back to Camelon in 1958. It was a Stirling designer, Sandford Morley, who devised the famous Bluebird logo, which distinguished Alexander's Scottish bus fleet.

Stirling had a tradition of coach building. The oldest firm was that of William Kinross & Sons, Motor & Carriage Works, in business from 1802 until the 1960s. McEwen Stirling Perambulator Works, established on Abbey Road in 1861, was the oldest of Scotland's five pram works and exported rickshaws and other carriages. There is a pram retailer in the same premises today.

The Under-21 team of Gowanhill United Football Club in action. From the 1920s until the 1960s, Gowanhill was the Raploch team, taking their name from the Gowan or 'Gowling' Hill beside Stirling Castle, which was the playground of Raploch residents. The name 'Gowling' is said to mean 'the place of lamentation' as the Heading or Beheading Stone is situated there. Gowanhill's most famous player was Billy Bremner (1942–1997); he gained admission to the team at the age of thirteen in 1956, although the manager was reluctant to have him on account of his small size. Bremner signed for Leeds Utd in 1958 and went on to win 55 caps for Scotland.

Gowanhill Community Association, photographed in 1950s. The Association had a busy programme of events, as well as running a drama club. Their interpretation of the meaning of 'gowan' as a daisy is evident from the large appliquéd daisies on their tablecloth.

The Heading or Beheading Stone on the Gowan Hill, overlooking Stirling. It was put to regular use by the Stewart kings.

In the nineteenth century the Heading Stone was in danger of being lost as it was being used as a butcher's block at premises near the Old Bridge, but the Stirling Natural History and Archaeological Society rescued it and secured it on the Gowan Hill. The plinth and protective cage was designed by the architect John Allan in 1887. The two cannons were purchased from the Castle in 1904.

A view of Stirling from Gowan Hill, looking across the windings of the Forth to the Abbey Craig and the National Wallace Monument. The photograph was taken for the proprietors of the Forthvale Works of the Rubber Company of Scotland, the large works with the chimney situated to the upper left of the Old Bridge on its north side. In 1857, a slaughterhouse and the poorhouse (now Orchard Hospital), were built on the south side of the Old Bridge.

The Rubber Company of Scotland, established in the early twentieth century, made everything from hot-water bottles to gloves. It took over the premises of the earlier Forthvale Woollen Mills at Bridgehaugh and, in the 1970s and 1980s, it was owned by H.K. Porter. Two buy-outs later saw it closed in 1992, and this building was demolished in January 1994.

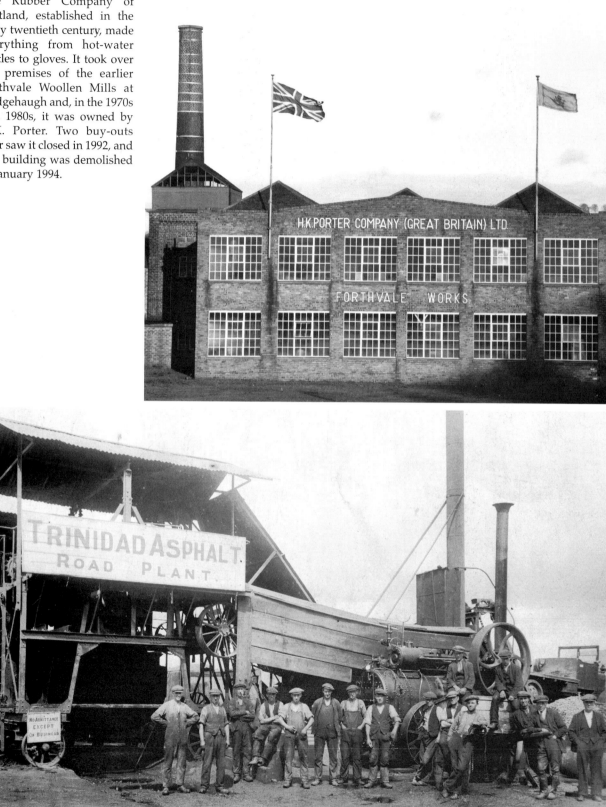

The Limner and Trinidad Asphalt Company which came to Stirling in the 1920s was also sited at Bridgehaugh. The resurfacing of all of the major roadways with asphalt cut the noise, dust and dirt of the old-fashioned road surfaces, making it one of the most popular innovations of the twentieth century. This photograph was taken in 1926 and shows Peter Faucet, foreman, on the extreme right. The fumes from the tarry boilers were thought to have curative properties, and in the 1940s children with whooping cough and other ailments were brought here to inhale the fumes.

Stirling Castle dominates the landscape from every aspect. There were prehistoric fortifications here, and from mediaeval times the fortress protected the bridge of Stirling, the crossing point over the River Forth on the main route north and south through the surrounding boggy marshes. The neat fields in the foreground were created in the eighteenth century, through the stripping of the peat bogs by the 'moss lairds'. The Stirling–Dunfermline railway line follows the banks of the river. This was constructed between 1850 and 1853, closed in 1968, and partially reopened in 2008. Forthvale Woollen Mill is in the centre of this photograph, which dates from about 1890.

Until the present footbridge was built in 1935, the village of Cambuskenneth was accessed from Stirling by boat. The ferry man's house is on the right-hand side. Isolated on a loop of the River Forth, the village was popular with artists and many of the 'Glasgow Boys' spent their summers here in the period 1880–1910. The village at that time consisted of a couple of streets surrounded by farmland.

The fifteenth-century stone Old Bridge served as the main crossing point over the Forth. Built *c*.1450, it took the place of the wooden bridge of eight pillars which was the scene of William Wallace's famous victory on 11 September 1297. The foundations of these pillars were examined on the river bed in 1995–1998. The Old Bridge still stands but was replaced as a main access route by Robert Stevenson's bridge of 1833.

Stirling Castle from the Back Walk, *c*.1890. During the period when the Castle was run by the army, from around 1700 until 1964, the trees and vegetation on the castle rock were kept to a minimum for security purposes and since the 1960s a forest has grown up on this side. In the century between 1830 and 1930, the trees that were allowed to grow on the hillside fed the Mauchline Ware wooden souvenir industry and often the items, although made in Mauchline, carried the legend 'made from wood grown on the slopes of Stirling Castle'. Once popular in tourist shops throughout the district, these are now collectors' items.

The Back Walk was laid out at the expense of William Edmonstone of Cambuswallace in 1724, about a century and a half before the public parks movement secured green spaces in other cities. The Walk continues around the escarpment with spectacular views to the Touch Hills and the Trossachs.

A photographer at work on the Back Walk, near the Butt Well. The beauties of the Back Walk were extolled in Stirling's earlier histories and guidebooks and for generations it was a major tourist attraction as well as the favoured walkway of locals. It has been less appreciated over the last fifty years as the emphasis of local tourism has been switched to other, revenue-generating attractions.

The Butt Well, on the Back Walk, is one of the ancient wells of Stirling. Although the structure is still in place, the water has long since ceased to flow. The Butts were the designated area for safely practising archery, and many Scottish burghs had butts in the fifteenth and sixteenth centuries. In the Stirling Burgh Records of 15 April 1676 it was noted that 'the sport of archerie was almost decayed' and the town treasurer was instructed to spend £24 Scots on a silver arrow as a competition prize for Stirling's archers. A prize of a silver goblet was added in 1686.

In this photograph, Mr McIlvean, shoemaker, is seated with his terrier. The well was last used by the homeless squatters who occupied the Nissen Huts in the area in the years after the Second World War.

This photograph was taken by Alexander Crowe, 'portrait and landscape photographer' of 33 Murray Place, Stirling. A pioneer photographer, he began life as a cabinetmaker and built his own cameras. He worked for James Valentine and the prints marked 'JV' in this book may have been taken by him. He settled in Stirling in 1859, and went into partnership with William Rodger in 1872. Crowe and Rodger were Stirling's best-known photographers for a generation.

King James V's Palace building in Stirling Castle and, on the far right, part of the Great Hall. Both Palace and Hall were used for military purposes until 1964. This photograph dates from around 1914 and the horse-drawn vehicles are delivery carts.

A military guard of honour, near Argyll's Lodging in Castle Wynd. The soldiers are awaiting a cortege, headed for the Valley Cemetery on the left, out of view. This photograph appeared on a postcard sent from Jack Thomas to his mother in South Wales on 20 April 1916; it reads, 'Can you pick me out in this crowd? This is when we were waiting for the corpse of the Gordon Highlander who was drowned. I think I told you about it in the letter. Fondest love etc., Jack'.

Military funerals were something of a spectacle, with a lament played on the pipes and a volley fired over the coffin. Pupils of Stirling High School sometimes played truant to watch the ceremonies from the Ladies' Rock in the Cemetery.

This battalion of troops is marching the well-worn road from Stirling Station to Stirling Castle. Again, the photograph appeared on a postcard, the reverse of which is dated 29 April 1916. Addressed to Lizzie Drummond at 16 Raploch, it reads, 'Weekend cancelled. Have been confined to barracks. Waiting further orders. It's funny but it's true. With kindest regards from yours sincerely, SZ'.

The railway came to Stirling in 1848, with the expansion of the Scottish Central Railway between Glasgow, Edinburgh and Perth. The Scottish Central became part of the Caledonian Railway in 1866.

Stirling Railway Station was built in 1913–1915, to the design of Glasgow architect James Miller, replacing the earlier building of 1855. With its crow stepped gables, castellated façade and light interior with sweeping curves, it is regarded as one of the loveliest of the surviving Scottish railway stations of that period.

This photograph was taken from above the Arcade entrance, looking down Station Road in 1932. The Station Hotel is on the right. The business of Thomas Ross, Monumental Mason, on the left, survived until the 1990s.

A 4-4-0 'Oban bogie' (No. 182) designed by George Brittain for the Caledonian Railway Company.

The locomotive is shown facing south in the down station sidings next to the former platform 1 at Stirling Station. The bridge to Riverside is in the right background. The buildings in the left background are on the site of the soon-to-be-built Regal Cinema. The water tank was a familiar landmark at this location for many decades. No. 182, allocated new to Stirling, was rebuilt in March 1902 and was one of the last three withdrawn in 1930. In addition to the number on the tender and smokebox door, the LMS crest is on the cabside and therefore the locomotive is almost certainly in LMS crimson lake passenger engine livery, and the date is around 1923.

During the First World War, regiment after regiment was recruited in and processed through Stirling before being sent to fight in the trenches. The whole town was used for training and provisioning purposes. This party of soldiers are training with their horses in Victoria Square, King's Park. One of the men has the bit between his own teeth!

A military display in the middle of King Street during the First World War. The gun is labelled 'captured at Loos by 7th Division Sept. 25th 1915' (the first day of that battle). Showing enemy arms was not an uncommon practice and Stirling still displays six cannons captured at Sebastopol during the Crimean War – two in Broad Street, two at Cowane's Hospital, and two on the Gowan Hill.

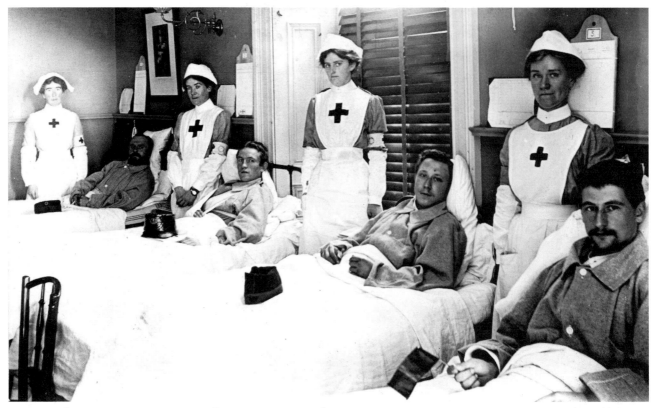

Red Cross hospital accommodation in the Stirling area. On the outbreak of war in 1914 plans to build a maternity hospital were deferred as all resources were needed to accommodate the wounded returning from battle. A maternity unit was later provided as part of the Stirling Royal Infirmary in 1928.

A recruitment office on the ground floor of the South Church, Murray Place, in 1914. The 'second half million' soldiers required for the army are mentioned on the poster on the left and veterans were employed to recruit young men prior to the introduction of conscription in 1916 (three million men enlisted during the first two years of the war).

Flag Day, 22 January 1916. The weather was so bad that the flag sellers had to take shelter in the Arcade between King Street and Murray Place. Note the directions to the pit, stalls and circle of the Arcade Theatre on the doors behind. This theatre was built in 1881/82, and had a name change in 1936, becoming the Alhambra. Music Hall and Variety were its specialities. It closed in the mid 1960s.

During the storm of 22 January 1916, some of the flag sellers took refuge in the Free North Church on Murray Place. This was built in 1853, after the congregation of the North Church had split during the Disruption ten years earlier.

The whole countryside around Stirling was used for military training and exercises during the two world wars and after. On 26 July 1916, this battalion was photographed crossing the Bannock Burn, fully equipped and with gun carriages.

Sports day, 1 June 1918, for the 5th Battalion of the Highland Light Infantry who were stationed in Cornton Camp (where Cornton Vale Prison is now). The corporal is putting the company mascot, the Shetland pony Harry, through his paces. Shetland ponies were favoured mascots of several Scottish regiments. The Argyll and Sutherland Highlanders had a succession of them, each named Cruachan, prior to their absorption into the Royal Regiment of Scotland in 2006.

During the Second World War, the Stirling area was also host to several prisoner-of-war camps. This is the Italian drama group of POW Camp 64 at Denny. This particular hut was used as a chapel, but was transformed into the Sala Roma theatre, with the wolf, symbol of Rome, above the proscenium. In the middle row, second from the right is scene painter Vincenzo Donnarumma, with technical director and playwright Vincenzo Tedeschi third from the right. Both acted as liaison officers with the British officers, distributing the four shillings weekly payment to the Italian prisoners working on local farms. The payment was no more than pocket money, which they spent on ice cream and cigarettes. The drawings from the walls of the adjacent German POW hut are in the Stirling Smith collections.

The Argyll and Sutherland Highlanders was Stirling Castle's resident regiment. This inspection, by Colonel-in-Chief Queen Elizabeth, took place as part of the centenary celebrations of the Battle of Balaklava in October 1954. These included a dramatic performance, with battle scenes re-enacted, in the Albert Halls. The scenery was painted by James Atterson D.A., art master at the High School. In 2004, the 150th anniversary was marked by lectures and a regimental visit to the battle site.

With Stirling used as both barracks and training ground for troops throughout the nineteenth century, and playing an important part in the organisation for two world wars in the twentieth century, the people of Stirling had a deep interest in the conduct and progress of the wars of the day. The old boys of the High School recalled their lessons being interrupted by the noise of gunfire as the soldiers trained, and the welcome successive half-day holidays in celebration of the Crimean battles of Alma, Balaklava, Inkerman and the fall of Sebastopol.

As Stirling Castle was a royal residence until 1603, many noble and wealthy families kept town houses in Stirling to be near the royal court. Mar's Wark, built at the head of Broad Street, was the greatest of these. Built in 1570–72 for the Earl of Mar, Regent of Scotland, and highly decorated with sculpture, quotations and armorial panels, it was rented as a workhouse by the burgh from 1783. It subsequently became ruinous and was reduced to two storeys by the time the replacement poorhouse, hospital and lunatic asylum opened in Union Street in 1856.

This image of the 1850s shows a two-storey vernacular building (long since demolished) sharing the gable of Mar's Wark on the right. This building sat within the grounds of the Georgian building known as the Valley Lodge, which still survives. It is likely that both were built from the materials of Mar's Wark. Local tradition maintains that Mar's Wark itself was built from stone robbed from Cambuskenneth Abbey after the Scottish Reformation.

The term *lodging* or *ludging* is usually applied to the town residence of a member of the aristocracy whose principal residence is elsewhere, and this building, known as Argyll's Lodging, is one of the finest surviving Renaissance palaces in Scotland. It was built in four phases, starting in the mid-sixteenth century, was extended by the poet Sir William Alexander of Menstrie, Earl of Stirling, and again by the ninth Earl of Argyll who owned it in the late seventeenth century. In the nineteenth century, it became a military hospital after the billeting of sick soldiers on the local population had ceased to be acceptable.

In the mid-twentieth century it became a youth hostel. After the development of Stirling Castle as a major heritage attraction, Argyll's Lodging was restored to its seventeenth-century splendour in 1997.

The Church of the Holy Rude, seen from near the top of St John Street, is one of the great surviving mediaeval churches of Scotland. Begun in 1456, it was the parish church of Stirling and was still unfinished at the time of the Reformation in 1560; as the external niches for statues were never filled, it remains so. The infant King James VI was crowned here on 29 July 1567.

On the right of the photograph is Stirling Boy's Club, a facility created by Major Crum (1872–1955) in 1929 for boys who were not attracted to formal organisations such as the Scouts. The architect Eric Bell constructed it from traditional materials on the site of the old butter and poultry market and adorned it with mottos such as 'Keep Smiling' and 'Play the Game'. It is still used as a community centre. The building beyond has since been demolished and rebuilt, like most of the Top of the Town area.

Bruce of Auchenbowie's house, on the left of the photograph, is one of the few original houses to survive at the Top of the Town. It dates from the sixteenth century and Bruce was one of many noblemen who chose to reside in this part of the town. The forestair and the wooden structure on the first floor, precariously balanced on a pillar, have since been removed.

Cowane's Hospital was built through the bequest of John Cowane (died 1633), merchant, to house 'twelve decayed gildbrothers, burgesses and in-dwellers of the burgh.' It was designed by John Mylne, the royal master mason, and constructed between 1637 and 1648. The building is E-shaped in plan with attractive crow-stepped gables and adorned with a full-size statue of John Cowane. Affectionately known as 'Auld Staneybreeks', the statue is reputed to come alive every 1 January and dance a jig before returning to the plinth. The Cowane's Hospital Trust is a powerful charity in Stirling to this day. Although the building was never used as a poorhouse or hospital as intended, it has remained an important civic building. The Stirling Guildry has met there over the centuries. The cannons captured at Sebastopol in 1855 can be seen at the top of the steps. This photograph was taken by freelance press photographer A.D.S. MacPherson.

Broad Street, looking towards Mar's Wark at the top of the street. On the left is the Tolbooth or town house, rebuilt in 1704 to the plan of architect Sir William Bruce. It contained the courtroom, prison and burgh offices. Extended in 1785, it was supplemented by the acquisition of the Athenaeum at the head of King Street in 1875, and in 2002 it was converted into a space for music and the arts.

Most of the buildings in Broad Street were built for members of the aristocracy and the wealthier merchant classes. The markets were held in Broad Street, and the standard weights and measures were kept in the Tolbooth.

Antiquaries such as J.S. Fleming and James Ronald, who were able to inspect the interiors of some of the buildings in the early years of the twentieth century, have left written testimonies as to the quality of those buildings. By that time, the middle classes had left the old town for the new lower town to settle in the Allan Park, King's Park and Terraces areas. The old houses were sub-divided, over-crowded, lacking in sanitation, and became among the worst slums in Britain.

Looking down Broad Street to the junction with Bow Street, *c*.1918.

Below: The bottom of Broad Street, at its junction with St Mary's Wynd (on the left) and Bow Street (on the right). The shops and businesses on the ground floor of these tenement properties ensured that commerce was local and that the community was lively. From left to right are a sale room and pawn shop, a dairy, a grocer and spirit merchant, Notarangelo's ice cream and fish restaurant (see page 58), Stirling Co-operative, a joiner and undertaker, and three small shops. Note the condition of the roof above Notarangelo's Ice and Fish Restaurant; the ridge has sagged through lack of maintenance.

The only surviving building in this scene is the three-storey, three-dormered tenement left of centre, which is known as Darnley's House.

Right: A back court in Broad Street, 1953. The wooden tower for the water closets, grafted on to the earlier building, could be said to be the 1901 equivalent of the 2001 satellite dish. A brush-head wireless aerial has been tacked on to the wooden tower.

Below: The Tolbooth tower, photographed from a room in Darnley's House. That Darnley's House survived was due to the photographer David Stirling, then an employee in the Sanitary Department. He witnessed the unsuccessful attempts of the demolition crew who were trying to topple the gable; unlike those which surrounded it, Darnley's House was still solid and in good condition. Stirling raised the alarm with a number of government departments and the House was saved at the last minute on historic grounds, although the connection with Lord Darnley, husband of Mary Queen of Scots, is spurious.

Right: Mrs Ferguson, a resident of Broad Street. Images taken inside Stirling houses at that time are very rare and only a handful of interior photographs survive in public collections. The photographer was Minnie Dewar (1866–1948) who took it up as a business in the period 1910–1920 after the death of her husband, a pharmacist and picture framer.

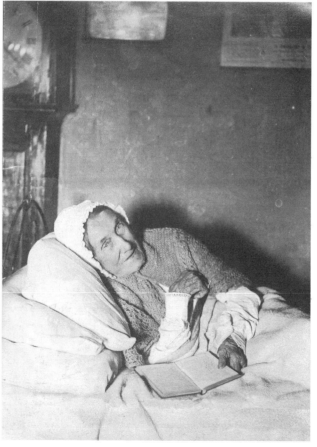

Above: Houses at 23 Broad Street, closed as unsafe in 1950. This photograph is from a sanitary inspector's album.

Provost James Plank with Sheriff McConachie proclaims the accession of Queen Elizabeth at the Cross, 6 February 1952. There was a full civic procession, involving the councillors, magistrates, Guildry and trades of Stirling. The new monarch was also proclaimed at the limits of the burgh and at important points, including the Castle esplanade and outside the municipal buildings in Corn Exchange.

The Market Cross, the traditional place of proclamation, has occupied four different locations in Broad Street over the last 200 years, usually being moved to accommodate changing traffic patterns. The unicorn on the top is known as the 'puggy'. In earlier times, members of the seven incorporated trades were called to arms in defence of the burgh when the Blue Blanket, their ancient banner, was unfurled at the Cross. Acts of defiance also took place; it was here the Articles of Union were burned on 4 December 1706.

The proclamation party of 1952, marching from the Tolbooth to the Albert Halls. With Provost James Plank are Sir Ian Bolton and Sheriff McConachie, preceded by Halberdiers Miller, Robertson and Wilson. The Halberdiers were the burgh officers who were the armed guard for the Provost and Magistrates. Their uniform was first detailed in July 1607, when it was ordered to be made from 'rid inglishe kaisar' (red English cashmere). The uniforms seen here are now in the Smith collections.

A photograph of the densely crowded housing between Spittal Street on the left and Baker Street on the right, taken from a back window of the Athenaeum building at the head of King Street. At the top left corner is the majestic structure of the High School of Stirling, begun in 1854 and extended in 1887–90.

It is difficult now to imagine the conditions that prevailed in this area in the nineteenth century. Even livestock suffered. In April 1887, for example, an outbreak of pleuro-pneumonia was recorded in Mr Ewing's byre in Baker Street. Of the twelve cattle there, seven were killed and buried, and five were sent to the dead meat market in Glasgow.

The filthy conditions in Stirling are described in graphic detail in the 1841 Poor Law Commissioners' Report on sanitation, and it was only after a serious cholera scare in 1872 that the decision was made to levy a charge for the construction of an adequate sewerage system.

The densely crowded backlands were reduced in the demolitions of the 1950s. An entire section of Baker Street was removed to create a green space, Baker Street Gardens, within the old town.

These three seventeenth-century houses with the crow-stepped gables at numbers 13–25 Baker Street were demolished in 1900. A date stone indicated that they were built in 1631. The shop in the centre building was occupied by Leathley, Fish and Fruit Merchant, who was a royal warrant holder and had several other shops in the town. The building on the left (number 13) had an inscribed stone which proclaimed 'HEIR I FORBEARE MY NAME OR ARMES TO FIX LEAST I OR MINE SHOULD SELL THOSE STONES AND STICKS'. This was a challenge to the Craigengelt family, who had fixed their coat of arms on the building on the extreme right, which is still extant. This stone is now in the Stirling Smith collection.

The Refreshment Rooms at number 25 served that purpose throughout the nineteenth century.

M'CULLOCH & YOUNG, LTD.
ING STREET (Opposite Top of Friars St.) STIRLING

LADIES' AND CHILDREN'S OUTFITTERS
and COMPLETE HOUSE FURNISHERS

Baker Street has always been a busy retail area. By 1933, the department store of McCulloch and Young Ltd had acquired all of the buildings at the foot of Baker Street and Spittal Street, a triangle of property with the Athenaeum building at its apex. The company advertised itself as 'Stirling's Largest Store' and the House Furnishing, Men's Wear, Drapery and China Departments were clearly marked on the line drawing in their advertisement.

This photograph was taken after the closing down sale in the 1960s. The buildings were demolished shortly afterwards and replaced by the present long concrete block.

This is the Spittal Street side of the McCulloch and Young triangle of property in King Street/Baker Street/Spittal Street. The white three-storey seventeenth-century building with the red pantile roof and cropped windows on the top floor, is an interesting contrast with the classically proportioned 1816 structure of the Athenaeum on its right. On the extreme right of the photograph is the 1899 red sandstone Clydesdale Bank building (architect, James Thomson), which is richly decorated with sculpted figures from Scottish history.

A rooftop view of Stirling, looking south from the Observatory Tower of the High School in Spittal Street. The Observatory, which is still used by members of the Stirling Astronomical Society, was gifted in 1890 by Sir Henry Campbell-Bannerman, MP for Stirling Burghs and Prime Minister of Great Britain. The distinctive half-timbered building with the bargeboards on the left is 55 Baker Street, designed by Stirling architect John Allan (1846–1922) in 1880.

A view looking up Spittal Street. On the left-hand side are three important public institutions. The Gothic building on the far left is Snowdon School for Girls, built as a Reformatory or Ragged School in 1855, certified as an Industrial School in 1864, and taken over by the Scottish Education Department from which it received its 'more euphonious sounding name' in 1929. Its chequered history can be traced through its annual reports, Register of Detention and Punishment Book, all in Stirling Council Archives. It still operates as a residential girls' school.

The classical building next door is the Commercial Bank, built in 1825, which later served as the first Stirling Royal Infirmary from 1874 until 1928. The premises are scheduled for hotel development.

At the top of the street is the 1887–90 phase of the High School of Stirling, with its Observatory Tower. The school's site, chosen in 1854, was that of the Stirling slaughterhouse, and the building of the school changed the nature of the street for the better. The school moved to Torbrex in 1962 and the building became a hotel in 1991, although the Stirling Astronomical Society still uses the observatory.

Spittal Street was named after Robert Spittal, tailor to King James IV, whose money funded a hospital for the Trades. It was previously known as 'the Back Row', a street which had many workshops and industrial premises. These were cleared in the nineteenth century for the public buildings seen here.

Another view from the Observatory Tower, this time looking north up Spittal and St John's Streets to the Church of the Holy Rude and the Castle. Some of these photographs are from the album of Walter Gillespie, Burgh Architect, who had the task of rebuilding the Top of the Town in the 1950s.

Baker Street, at the corner of Friars Street. The Bank of Scotland is on the right. The Star Hotel at 2 Baker Street was advertised in 1887 as '… under new management – cleaned, redecorated and painted throughout and is one of the most comfortable houses in Scotland. Gentlemen residents have the right of salmon fishing in the Forth, free.' It was demolished around 1902. The military parade would have been heading for the Castle.

Baker Street, at the junction of Friars Street, looking north, *c.*1938. Baker Street has always been a busy retail thoroughfare with a good mix of shops. On the extreme left is the big department store of McCulloch and Young. The tenement on the extreme right was built by the local architectural partnership of McLuckie and Walker in 1905, replacing the Star Inn. The ground floor is still a public house today.

Baker Street, looking south. On the right is a handsome, three-storey tenement with crow-stepped gables; it probably dated from the eighteenth century, but was cleared away in the demolitions of the 1950s. The half-timbered tenement at 55 Baker Street is by architect John Allan and still stands. In the centre distance is the Bank of Scotland building of 1833, designed by William Burn. As with many banks of that time, it was both business premises and a house for the banker. Grand social events are recorded during the tenure of Mr Brodie, Bank of Scotland agent in Stirling from 1833 to 1863.

Numbers 56–62 Baker Street, 1937. The gable was shored, prior to excavation for the purposes of a new sewer. It was found that the rock surface shelved steeply to a depth of seven feet in the middle of the gable. By February 1938, it was so unstable that a decision was made to demolish this building, although the wholesale demolition and rebuilding of Baker Street did not take place until the 1950s.

The top of Baker Street at its junction with Bow Street, 1938. These once-handsome tenements were by that time showing signs of neglect and, after the Second World War, the whole area was cleared.

Bow Street, looking south to the top of Baker Street. In the distance is the tower of the High School of Stirling. The children of the Grammar School on Castlehill were familiar with these shops in 'The Bow' before they moved to the High School in 1856, and there seemed to them to be little change in the shops in the 50-year period between 1838 and 1888. Businessman J.R. McArthur, speaking at a school prize giving ceremony in 1889, remarked on this but added 'the old school boy on seeing the present noble pile [i.e. of new school buildings], and the High School Prospectus for 1888/89 would be led to exclaim "This is not a change: it's a revolution".'

This, and more on the High School of Stirling, can be read in *Old Boys and their stories of the High School of Stirling* (1900), edited by J. Lascelles Graham.

A procession in the quadrangle of the High School of Stirling, *c*.1912. The exact occasion is not known, but an annual High School Festival was started in 1882 with the inauguration of the new south wing. Music and drama were important aspects of the event.

On 12 May 1856, the Grammar School pupils marched from Castlehill to their new High School in Academy Road. The centenary saw a re-enactment on 11 May 1956, with the pupils retracing their steps, worshipping in the Holy Rude, and visiting Cowane's Hospital and the Tolbooth *en route*. The biggest march was on 25 April 1962, when a thousand pupils moved out of Academy Road and across the burgh to the new High School building at Torbrex. The old school is now the Stirling Highland Hotel.

The east side of Spittal Street at the junction with Academy Road, looking towards the steep curve of Bow Street. The seventeenth-century building with the Glengarry Lodge public house was known as the Darrow Ludging. It has served many purposes in its time, including that of an Episcopal chapel and a china shop. It was completely restored in 1994. Most of the surrounding housing was cleared away in the 1950s.

Bow Street, partially cleared, in 1938. The street linked Baker Street with Broad Street and, in the nineteenth century, the Bow was narrow, enclosed, and notoriously dangerous for carriage traffic. Prior to Queen Victoria's visit in 1842, much practice was put in by William Ramsay of Barnton (1809–1850) MP, horseman and promoter of the Stirling Races, who was to drive the Queen on her visit. He drove up and down to the castle and round the Bow with a carriage and four horses. As a contemporary recalled, 'The ticklish part was in the Bow where the leaders at the sharp corner were out of sight of the driver . . . the cheering and firing were very trying for the horses . . . and it is said that Queen Victoria had tears of fright in her pretty eyes.'

The Baker Street Post Office was formerly the bookshop where the artist Sir George Harvey (1806–1876) was apprenticed in his youth, and he made drawings of the faces of children peering in the window with curiosity.

One hundred and twenty years later, another young queen comes down the newly rebuilt Bow, towards Baker Street, this time on foot. The informality of 1962 would not be possible today. Escorting Queen Elizabeth is Provost William MacFarlane Gray (1958–1964), a well-known accountant who served on the board of ITV, established the Stirling Festival, and brought many great orchestras to perform in Stirling. The dark-haired young councillor behind him is Ian Wyles, who was later Provost from 1984 to 1988.

The architect's plan for the reconstruction of Baker Street in the early 1950s. The idea was to follow the line of the old housing, and to retain the spirit of the historic buildings with the crow-stepped and Dutch gables. In charge of the project was Sir Frank Mears, but it fell to the newly appointed Burgh Architect, Walter Gillespie, to work out the details.

BAKER STREET CLEARANCE

The Baker Street clearance area, from the album of Walter Gillespie. The south side of Baker Street was largely demolished, along with parts of the north side of Spittal Street, leaving an opening for the present Baker Street Gardens. This provided a much-needed green lung in the upper town at that time, and for the first time, the frontage of the High School of Stirling could be seen from street level.

Below: On 7 December 1928 the Thistle Property Trust was formed with the aim of refurbishing and improving the historic buildings in order to provide decent and affordable family houses. These were for 'persons mainly of the working classes in Stirling and the neighbouring district'. The driving force behind the Trust was the Stirling branch of the National Council of Women, a continuation of the pre-War women's suffrage movement. This row at the Top of the Town was the first property purchased by the Thistle Property Trust.

Above: Mr Malley digging one of the Trust's allotments in the St John Street area at the Top of the Town. The initials and date 'TPT 1931' can be seen in the rustic fencing.

Provost John Duff, who served from 1932 to 1935, and Mrs Munro, planting a rowan tree in the garden of one of the Thistle Property Trust houses at the Top of the Town. Rowans were traditionally planted beside houses to ward off evil spirits.

Mr Walker, posing with the Thistle Property Trust arms on one of the refurbished buildings at the Top of the Town. The Trust's architect was Eric S. Bell (1884–1972), whose award-winning houses of 1936 still stand in Drip Road, Raploch.

In spite of the work of the Trust, the problems at the Top of the Town were later deemed too great to resolve without wholesale demolition. The Trust's interests were bought out by Stirling Burgh in 1952, and a comprehensive demolition policy was pursued.

Opposite: Some of the Thistle Property Trust tenants in 1932. The placards carry the logo of the Trust and the merry-go-round was installed as part of the improvements.

Annie Croall (1854–1927) (*inset*) was the daughter of Alexander Croall, the Smith's first curator. Deeply religious and compassionate, she set up the Stirling Children's Home after finding a baby abandoned in the Back Walk; the mother had gone into town for drink and had been arrested. Annie Croall started the Home in four rooms in Broad Street. It then moved to the Craigs, and it was some time before she acquired Whinwell, a mansion on the Gowan Hill, where the photograph above was taken. By 1900, thanks to public support, the Home was free of debt.

Some of the Whinwell Children on the steps of Whinwell. Annie Croall recounted her struggles in the annual reports and notably in *Fifty Years on a Scottish Battlefield 1873–1923*. The battlefield metaphor was a pertinent one in historic Stirling. On many occasions she was asked, 'Wherever do you get your children from? I'm sure there are no slums in Stirling or anywhere near it.' But in a barracks town like Stirling, poverty and social problems went hand in hand. On one occasion, near Stirling cemetery, she found a woman in a one-roomed house with five illegitimate children: 'a stunted, starved lad of twelve, a deformed creature of eight, a boy aged six, almost blind, a wee lassie of four, emaciated and cowed, and a starving, blind baby.'

A school class in the Stirling Children's Home. Annie Croall rescued children from impossible situations. One family of children, aged eight, five and two, had been sleeping out on the Gowan Hill with their mother, a homeless prostitute. Another child, 20 months old, was found living off scraps on the floor of a common lodging house in St Mary's Wynd. Annie Croall took these traumatised children and gave them food, clothing and a loving environment. 'Truly, Miss Croall is a mother in Israel,' wrote a correspondent in the *Scottish Reformer* in 1908.

Like many schools of its kind and time, the Stirling Children's Home trained girls for domestic service and had an emigration policy for both sexes, sending some children abroad from the age of thirteen or fourteen. The Home was supported by a local Dorcas society who made the clothing, local merchants who provided food, and hundreds of local cash donations from individuals. These were meticulously detailed in the annual reports. Stirling Children's Home was taken over by the Aberlour Child Care Trust in 1980 and Whinwell House was subsequently demolished.

Opposite, clockwise from top left:
Number 80 St Mary's Wynd,
1920. This wynd, off Broad
Street, led to Bridge Street, the
main exit from Stirling, north
across the Old Bridge. It also
contained some of the town's
worst overcrowding and living
conditions.

Another view of 80 St Mary's
Wynd from the bottom of the
entry. These images are from the
album of a Sanitary Inspector,
probably John Fyfe who served in
that capacity from 1901 until
1941. St Mary's Wynd itself was
only fourteen feet wide and this
long narrow street was punctuated
with a warren of entries, closes
and backlands, and had primitive
sanitation at best.

St Mary's Wynd, looking towards
Broad Street, in the early 1920s.

Number 38 St Mary's Wynd,
showing a common street well,
downstream from an outside
toilet.

Top Left: Five children from
8 St Mary's Wynd, photographed
by the Stirling Sanitary Inspector.

Centre left: Number 14 St John
Street, looking towards the back
properties of 11 Broad Street.

Bottom left: Number 14 St John
Street, looking towards the back
of 10 St John Street.

Below: Number 14 St John Street,
looking towards 17 Broad Street.

Notarangelo's ice cream and chip shop and the Stirling Co-operative Society in Bow Street, photographed in the 1920s. The properties above Notarangelo's had been closed on account of the sagging roof.

Brock's public house and Welsh the grocer in Broad Street. Eddie Welsh was blind, but knew all the different coins by touch. This building contained the 'Long Close' through to St Mary's Wynd.

When this building was demolished, an overmantle painting of Stirling Castle was uncovered on the top floor. A large relieving arch, two storeys above Brock's pub was also revealed.

A fireplace wall in the first-floor back room of 113 Baker Street. The crowned thistle and vase of roses were in lime plaster. There was a matching vase of roses on the other side, but it was destroyed by a workman attempting to remove it before a photograph could be taken. The exterior of the building had a date stone of 1673 and the initials RR and CA. Numerous historical features were destroyed in the demolition of the upper town.

Demolition in St John Street, 1950. Note the painting above the fireplace.

One of the finest viewpoints in Stirling is from the fifteenth-century tower of the Church of the Holy Rude. Until the 1950s, public access was provided for a penny. The photographer has included part of the Valley Cemetery, Valley Lodge House (the white building, right foreground), the Old Grammar School (nearest left to Valley Lodge House), and the Castle esplanade in this shot.

The purchase and laying out of the ground of the Valley Cemetery just below the Castle was the munificent gift of the Drummond family, who were seedsmen and agricultural machinery manufacturers in Stirling. The first burial in the new cemetery was in 1857. The Valley was previously an area of rough ground where travelling shows exhibited, and had also been the scene of incidents of drunkenness and disorder. The deliberate change of the landscape into a place of instruction, contemplation and biblical education brought about the total transformation of a very rough place. The Drummond family evidently regarded the cemetery development as 'The Star of Snowdon', *Snowdon* being the ancient word for Stirling and the Star being the means by which the people of Stirling would be guided.

The Star Pyramid or Salem Rock at the head of the Valley Cemetery has numerous biblical references inscribed, the chief of which is Isaiah, Chapter 40: 'Prepare ye the way of the Lord, make straight in the desert a highway for our God. Every valley shall be exalted, and every mountain and hill shall be made low: and the crooked shall be made straight, and the rough places plain . . . All flesh is grass . . . but they that wait upon the Lord shall renew their strength; they shall mount up with wings as eagles; they shall run, and not be weary; and they shall walk and not faint.' The chapter is a biblical manual for the creation of Stirling's cemetery.

Note the stone balls at the foot of the Star Pyramid, both of which originally had cast-iron eagles to match the text. This photograph was taken between 1920 and 1930, according to the tombstone dates in the foreground. The other eagle has since disappeared too.

The Cemetery is laid out around seven statues. At its heart are these three: John Knox, leader of the Reformation of the Scottish church in 1560, Andrew Melville, who continued his work and published the *Second Book of Discipline*, and Alexander Henderson, of the third generation of the Reformed Church of Scotland, who led the great Glasgow General Assembly of 1628 which proclaimed Christ as the head of the Church.

In effect the seven statues illustrate the history of the Church of Scotland from 1560 to the nineteenth century. The statues were specified and financed by William Drummond (1793–1868) and made by the Edinburgh sculptor Alexander Handyside Ritchie (1804–1870).

Right: A view from the Ladies' Rock, possibly so-called on account of the ladies of the Castle using it as the place to view the tournaments and games that were once held in the Valley. The place name might also be an older, pre-Reformation reference to the Virgin Mary.

Below left: The Virgin Martyrs sculpture represents the sacrifice of Margaret MacLachlan and Margaret Wilson of Wigtown, who were staked out in the Solway and drowned by the tide on 11 May 1685 for refusing to swear an oath abjuring their covenanting beliefs. (The freedom of Agnes Wilson, Margaret's younger sister, was purchased by their father.) The sculptor Ritchie was proud of this group and the Edinburgh public viewed it in his studio in March 1859, prior to the installation in Stirling. The dedication of the group was done with great ceremony and each female member of the Drummond family wore commemorative enamel and pearl brooches, commissioned for the occasion.

Centre: A Virgin Martyrs brooch, known as 'the Star of Snowdon Purity Brooch', one of three in the Smith's collection. Snowdon is a literary name for Stirling, first used by the poet Sir David Lindsay in the sixteenth century. The brooch has the cross and crown of martyrdom, the laurel leaves of victory, three forget-me-not flowers in memory of the three accused women, and the pearl of purity, which is also symbolic of the name Margaret.

Right: As the Virgin Martyrs sculpture was in marble, it required the extra protection of a canopy. This was designed by the architect J.T. Rochead, who had just won the competition to design the National Wallace Monument on Abbey Craig, and installed in the 1860s. The casting was made by the Sun Foundry, Glasgow.

The route from south to north through Stirling in the eighteenth century was across the Old Bridge of Stirling, built in the fifteenth century. Access from St Ninian's Road to the Bridge involved climbing up Baker Street or the Back Row (as St John Street was then known) to Broad Street and St Mary's Wynd, then following the long road downwards. This changed when a much-needed new bridge, designed by Robert Louis Stevenson's grandfather, was built across the Forth not far from the Old Bridge in 1835.

The new road from St Ninians to the new bridge was laid out in the 1830s and was named Murray Place after local landowner John Murray of Polmaise. The traffic was able to avoid the steep braes of the old town, and Murray Place quickly became a fashionable shopping street as well as the direct north-south route. The residential tenement flats were occupied by those who could afford to move out of the Old Town. By the 1860s, Murray Place had several hotels for the growing tourist trade. On the right is the Waverley Temperance Hotel, and beyond it is the County Hotel and two others.

A view from further down Murray Place. The church with the square tower and Romanesque arches is the North Church (built in 1842), so named because the Holy Rude Church had been split into two congregations, the East Church and the West Church, since the time of the Reverend James Guthrie in the 1650s. A third minister was appointed on the creation of a third congregation in 1731, and in 1842 this became the North Church when the three congregations were formally separated. The North Church congregation moved to a new building in Braehead in 1971, when this building was demolished. The neighbouring Baptist Church, on the left, was demolished at the same time, and its congregation moved into the South Church on the other side of the street.

Murray Place, looking south. On the left is the Post Office, a handsome building of 1895, large for the town, but built to accommodate the huge postal business of the Drummond Tract Enterprise (see page 68). It was closed in 2008. Beyond it is the three-storey Royal Bank of Scotland, and on the opposite side, at the foot of Friars Street the three-storey block is the Commercial Bank of Scotland Ltd. The great spire of the South (now the Baptist) Church is beyond. The industrial building in the distance, in Orchard Place, is the motor and carriage works of Provost James Thomson, a business established in the 1830s which lasted more than a century. Its nearest rival was William Kinross and Sons, carriage makers to Queen Victoria, who latterly operated in nearby Port Street.

Left: This fine Italianate building at numbers 80–82 Murray Place was built as the Edinburgh and Glasgow Bank in 1854/55 by architect John Dick Peddie. It is at present a branch of the Royal Bank of Scotland. Murray Place and Barnton Street were developing as a prestigious business area in the 1850s and 60s.

Below: The building on the right is the County Club, on the corner of Murray Place and Station Road. It was a social and business centre run on behalf of Stirlingshire's landowners. Conveniently situated near the railway station, it had rooms for those visiting Stirling on business. The annual County Club Ball was one of the highlights of the Stirlingshire social calendar. The building was demolished in the 1960s.

Trinity Episcopal Church on the corner of Barnton Street and Maxwell Place was built in 1843 and demolished in 1878, when the demand for shops in this part of the town was pressing. Messrs MacEwen, Stirling's biggest and most successful grocery company, bought the distinctive corner site and built the four-storey tenement with ground floor shops which is visible on the left of the previous photograph, and which still stands. The Episcopal congregation moved to their present church in Dumbarton Road. On the left can be seen Viewfield Church, built as a Free Church in 1860 on the site of an Anti-Burgher Meeting House of 1752. In 1929 it became part of the Church of Scotland.

Barnton Street is a continuation of Murray Place. This photograph was taken from the back of Friars Street, before the construction of the west side of Barnton Street in about 1880. On the left are the distinctive County Buildings, completed in 1876. The faint outline of the Wallace Monument on Abbey Craig can be seen in the distance.

The County Buildings (now the Sheriff Court), built in Viewfield Place, off Barnton Street, to the 1864 design of Thomas Brown, and modified by Wardrop and Reid in 1874–76. A civic and military event is in progress at the gates.

Barnton Street, 1913. On the left is one of Henderson's Argyll charabancs (registration M5378). Henderson Brothers of Barnton Street licensed three 16hp Argylls in June 1908 for private hires. In the centre is one of Gardner's Yellow Peril charabancs, registration LC7316. Note the variety of shops, with a boot shop, Buttercup Dairy, piano shop, tearoom and garage visible on the left. The spire of Viewfield Church is in the centre.

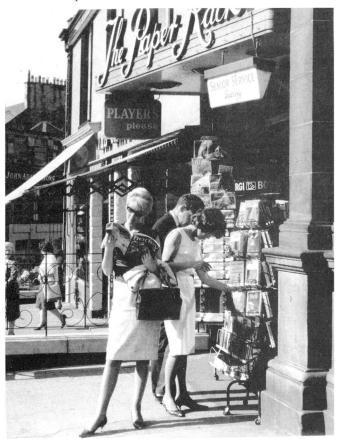

Twenty-year-old Valerie Robbie of Bridge of Allan was captured reading her magazine, at the Paper Rack on Murray Place, by photographer A.D.S. MacPherson in 1963. Note the tobacco advertising; at that time John Player's cigarette factory in Kerse Road was a major employer in the town.

King Street, Stirling.

King Street connected the Old Town to the new Murray Place. It was formerly known as Quality Street, but its name was changed in honour of King George IV around the time of his visit to Scotland in 1822. The building on the right was the

headquarters of the Drummond Tract Depot, another enterprise of the family responsible for the Valley Cemetery. It was designed in 1863 by Hay of Liverpool, who were the favoured architects of the Free Church and who also designed Snowdon School and the High School in Spittal Street. The Drummond Tract Depot began with Peter Drummond's temperance pamphlet campaign of 1848. Between then and its closure in 1980, an estimated 845 million items had been published and distributed, 475 million free of charge. Drummond magazines, pamphlets and religious tracts were issued worldwide, and the town still benefits from money made available for certain causes by the Drummond Trust today. Their *Stirling Annuals* were popular and valued seasonal gifts for children. The angel sculptural group above the first-floor window of the building, and the heads of the leaders of the Protestant Reformation above each of the windows on the ground floor, were removed by later owners after the

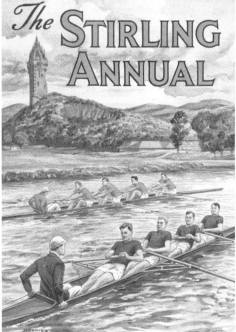

Drummond Trust Depot relocated to larger premises in Dumbarton Road. Since then the building has housed a number of banks, and is at present a clothing shop.

The Golden Lion Hotel, halfway up the street on the right-hand side dates to the 1760s and still functions as a popular central hotel. Robert Burns stayed here in August 1787 and inscribed his 'Stirling Lines', lamenting the condition of the town, on one of the window panes.

The Golden Lion Hotel, 6 King Street, *c*.1920. It suffered from the fire which destroyed the Drummond family's seed merchant premises in Murray Place in August 1949, losing eight rooms, the ballroom, and Robert Burns's 'Stirling Lines' glass. One of the hotel guests died of a heart attack. The building was repaired in 1949/50 and restored again in 1994.

Within the Golden Lion building were the premises of R.S. Shearer and Son, booksellers, stationers and printers, and publishers of *Shearer's Illustrated Guide to Stirling*. Their book bindery and stationer's works were in nearby Port Street.

The Golden Lion Staff Dance, *c*.1950. The General Manager, Eddie Adams, is presenting a prize. Numerous Stirling businesses and organisations held annual staff dances in the hotel at this time. It has never lost its character as a busy, well-loved Stirling institution.

Below left: This little building, which was tucked in beside the North Church in Murray Place, housed the picture and art gallery of Eneas Mackay and Son and faced their main premises, a single-storey newsagents' shop at 43 Murray Place, on the other side of the street. Mackay's was a Stirling publishing house of international significance. Their offices were a stone's throw from the Drummond Tract Depot and R.S. Shearer and Son. Eneas Mackay Senior (1860–1922) was from Inverness, had an interest in Gaelic literature and culture, and published Scottish books which sold worldwide. His son was in business with Jamieson Munro, which eventually became the Stirling Observer Press. The publishers Drummond, Shearer, Mackay and Munro worked in co-operation in Stirling. Publishing houses apart, Stirling had nine bookshops and two binderies in 1886. Today it can only sustain one or two bookshops.

Above: The *Stirling Observer* tenement still stands in Murray Place. It was built by Eneas Mackay, replacing the newsagents' shop at 43 Murray Place where his business began in 1882. It became a *Stirling Observer* branch in the 1920s, and the tenement was known as 'Observer Corner' as late as the 1970s.

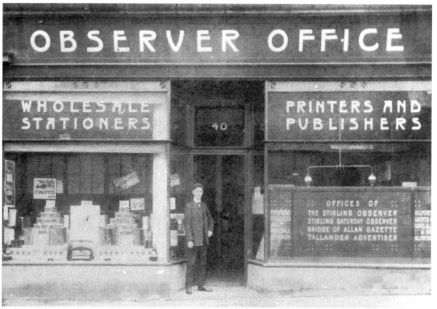

Left: The offices of the *Stirling Observer* Press have been in Upper Craigs since 1880. The paper was founded in 1836 and is now part of the Scottish and Universal Newspapers group. Stirling had three other newspapers: the *Stirling Journal* (1820–1971), the *Stirling Advertiser* (founded 1828; it merged with the Journal in 1833), and the *Stirling Sentinel* (1888–1955).

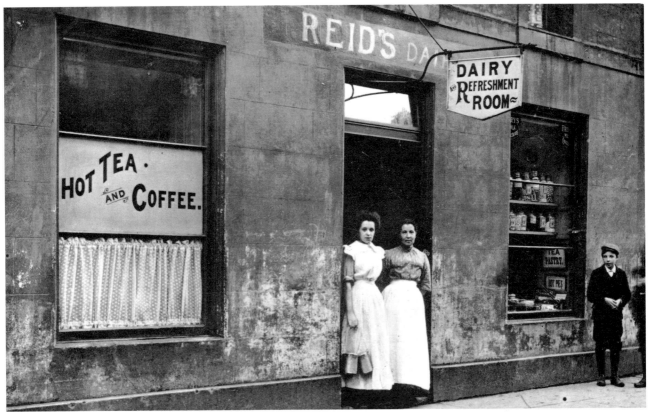

Reid's Dairy Refreshment Room, run by Mrs Stanley at 22 Upper Craigs, near the *Observer* office. In the 1820s, the Craigs area was a wilderness, and some of the more noxious industries, like the tan pits used by the Skinners' Incorporation, were at the far end of town on land known as 'the Skinners' mailing'. Cotton and carpet weaving was also carried out here. The area was well developed by the 1840s, with a mixture of housing, business and industry.

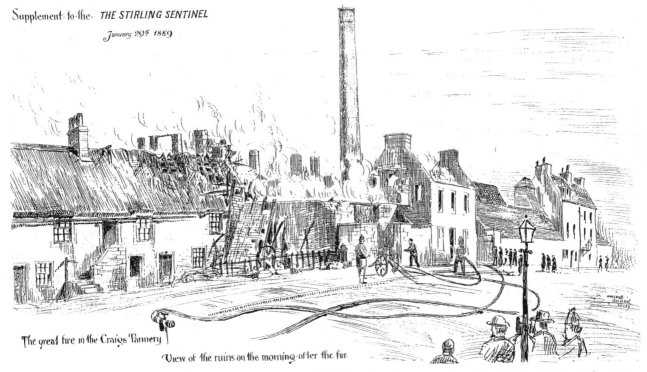

Supplement to the **THE STIRLING SENTINEL**

January 29th 1889

The great fire in the Craigs Tannery

View of the ruins on the morning after the fire

Photographs of the industries in the Craigs area are rare. This line drawing comes from the *Stirling Sentinel*. The Craigs Tannery belonged to Robert Gillies, and Craigs House – built as his father's residence in 1815 – stood opposite. This is presently a boutique hotel, and was previously a bank, a Masonic temple, and before that the home of the Templeton family who operated a carpet factory on the Burgh Muir. Parts of that factory are also still extant.

James Gray and Company, seed merchants, had their headquarters in Upper Craigs. In this photograph from the 1940s are some of the staff with a prize-winning horse. The company was established in 1865 and achieved a worldwide reputation for the quality of its seeds. It ceased trading in 1984. Like Drummond & Sons, they had a big export market for their produce.

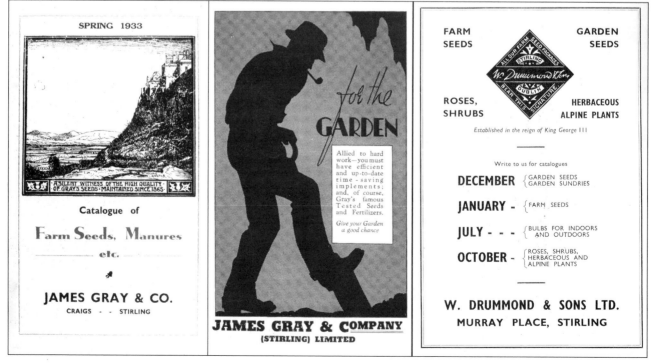

Craigs School was built in George Street in 1872 to serve the rapidly expanding population of the Craigs and Burghmuir areas. The Education (Scotland) Act of 1872 introduced compulsory education for children aged five to thirteen and the resulting new schools, such as Craigs, were governed by the School Board system to which people stood for election. A changing population and roads system saw Craigs School demolished in 1973, and the site is now presently occupied by the multi-storey Wellgreen car park.

ST. RINGAN'S CHAPEL WELL
(INTERIOR)

Wellgreen is at the back of the Craigs, and at the heart of it is St Ninian's Well, a spring of pure water associated with the sixth-century saint who brought Christianity to Scotland.

The photograph below was taken in the 1970s, when most of the industrial and residential buildings were being demolished to make way for the present Wellgreen business and car parks. In 1737 Stirling burgh decreed that it was 'very necessary that a common washing house be built at St Ninian's Well for the use of the inhabitants' and the oblong shape in the foreground is the remaining ground storey of that structure.

The Wellgreen was considered to be common property, and the first Stirling Highland games were held here in July 1870. By 1880, the area was feued out and the development was so intense that in 1888 a visiting antiquarian measured and drew the Well, fearing that it would be built over. The well is still extant in the middle of Wellgreen car park.

Allister McDonald (1923–2007) lived all of his life in the Craigs area of Stirling. From about 1970 until 2000, he maintained a trout hatchery in the sheltered spring of St Ninian's Well as his personal contribution to the conservation of brown trout. He tended trout eggs there and raised the hatched fry, releasing them into the River Forth. As a boy he went in the boats of the old salmon fishers on the River Forth. His working life was spent as a coachbuilder with Alexander's Buses in Raploch, and he waterproofed the inside of St Ninian's Well with discarded bus metal.

Traditional salmon fishers on the River Forth in the period 1880–1900. This photograph is one of a series taken by Sergeant McKenzie of the Argylls and a contemporary note states that the men were 'Mr McGlasson's fishermen'.

This is the first house to be have been built in what is now Melville Terrace and it was constructed by John Murray (1774–1861) of Livilands in the early 1800s. At the front, it had a straight sight line to St Ninian's Well, reduced to the present narrow Wellgreen Lane when Pitt Terrace was constructed (so the well can no longer be seen). This photograph was taken by Isabella Murray Wright, granddaughter of the builder, in about 1890. The garden was reduced in size to make way for the Peter Memorial Church (now St Columba's Parish Church), built in 1902.

The Wolf Craig building, 42 Port Street, designed by architect John Allan (1866–1922) in 1897/98. This was one of the first buildings in Scotland to be built on a steel frame, and the grocery store of Robertson and MacFarlane was the first emporium in Stirling to be lit with electric lighting. The building had its own electricity generator. A niche at first floor level has a sculpture of the legendary wolf, which howled and alerted the townspeople of a Viking raid, earning a place on the burgh insignia.

On the opposite side of the street is one of the major stores of D. & J. MacEwen & Co., an early grocery chain which began in Broad Street over 200 years ago and branched out all over the county, even as far north as Inverness. They were major importers of grain, animal feed, fertiliser and fine china tea – most of it through Stirling Harbour. The company still exists, but not in the retail business. Below is one of the fleet of lorries which stocked the shops of D. & J. MacEwen & Co. in the 1920s.

Stirling Harbour in the early 1900s. Before the Union of 1707, trade was mainly with the ports of the Baltic and the Netherlands, but with the opening of the American market Glasgow and the West Coast became more significant. The military had exclusive use of the harbour during the two world wars.

The middle class Victorian suburb of King's Park is often described as a 'railway suburb'. The laying out and building of the large family houses was given impetus by the introduction of the railway in 1848. Glasgow businessmen could afford to live in the clean air of Stirling, travelling to work by carriage and train. This photograph was taken from 7 Park Terrace, looking towards Glebe Crescent, by Isabella Murray Wright who lived in the house between 1860 and 1887.

New housing under construction at Victoria Place in King's Park. The photograph is by Sergeant McKenzie and dates from about 1880. In the foreground can be seen the outline of the former racetrack, the chief promoter of which was William Ramsay of Barnton (1809–1850), MP for Stirling. He financed the Stirling Gold Cup, and during his lifetime it was thought that Stirling would become the Doncaster of Scotland. The area became the course of Stirling Golf Club in 1869.

The opening of the new extended golf course on King's Park in July 1912, a remodelling of the course of 1869. Mrs Irvine Robertson is driving off from the first tee, opposite the clubhouse in Victoria Place. This was the first occasion on which women of the Stirling Ladies Golf Club were able to play the full course, except for Saturday afternoons and summer evenings, and unless playing in a mixed foursome. The clubhouse suffered from subsidence and was demolished after the current clubhouse was built in Queen's Road in 1962.

King's Park has played host to a variety of sports. At the front are the prizewinners of the Ariel Club, most of them Boy Scouts, pictured just before the First World War.

The back of this photograph is inscribed 'sledging in King's Park Saturday last. M. Dewar Arcade'. The photographer Minnie Dewar's images are quite distinctive. This and the upper photograph were taken for the press. She was in business at 33 The Arcade in 1914/15. Her work can also be seen on page 40.

Kings Park Football Club was formed in 1875. This team photograph of 1936 was issued as a 'photocard' by the Ardath Tobacco Company.

Left to right in the back row are J. Haggart, R. Baird (Captain), J. Milton, T. Fowler, J. Strathie and J. Laird.

In the front row, left to right, are H. McPherson, W. Hillan, R. Bryce, D. Miller and D. Rintoul.

From 1887, King's Park FC colours were cardinal red and white. Broad red and white striped shirts, white shorts and red hose were worn in the period 1926–1936. In 1938/39, narrower stripes and striped hose were adopted.

King's Park Football Club, sited at Annfield, was destroyed by one of the two German bombs which fell on Stirling on 20 July 1940. The stand, terracing, press room, dressing room and offices were wrecked and a crater eighteen feet deep was left in the ground. There were some casualties, but no fatalities. A goldfish in one of the wrecked houses had its tail blown off, but revived and lived when some drops of brandy were administered! Plate glass windows in Stirling town centre were broken. After the war, the club was reborn as Stirling Albion.

For many decades King's Park was used for open-air political meetings, and before the land was secured on behalf of the National Trust for Scotland at Bannockburn the annual Bannockburn Day Rally was held here. On the platform is the Scottish Nationalist, Robert Bontine Cunninghame Graham, who visited on 23 June 1928.

An Anderson shelter in the garden of 21 Albert Place, the home of the McLaren family in 1939 when this photograph was taken. Anderson shelters were designed and distributed to families with gardens at the request of Home Secretary John Anderson at the start of the Second World War, and were used during bombing raids. The standard shelter was six feet high, six and a half feet in length, four and a half feet wide, made of fourteen sheets of corrugated iron, buried to a depth of four feet and covered with at least fifteen inches of soil. The shelter in this photograph is obviously many times that size. Norman McLaren (1914–1987), the pioneer of film animation, was born and grew up in 21 Albert Place. He produced over 60 films and won over 200 awards for his work.

Top: This mansion, designed by F. & M. Mackison, is at 21 Victoria Place. In 1919 it became a private 'prep' boarding school for boys aged five to eleven and was named Hurst Grange. It had 40 pupils in 1922, expanding to about 100 in the 1960s. Among its distinguished former pupils is the Scottish novelist James Robertson. In 1975 the school amalgamated with the Beacon School for Girls in Bridge of Allan to become Beaconhurst Grange School. This house, now known as Hurstgrange, is presently a private residence. The railings disappeared in the Second World War salvage drive.

Centre: Cliffbank at 32–34 Albert Place is a handsome double villa built by architect John Allan as his own home (he lived in number 34). Allan designed many of the houses in King's Park, as well as a number of distinctive buildings in the town centre.

Bottom: Batterflats House on Polmaise Road is one of the largest and most distinctive mansions in Stirling. Built in 1893–95 for one of the Drummond family, it was designed by architect John Allan and originally had six acres of grounds. Like other Drummond family houses, it has a tower.

In 1929, the house was bequeathed to the Church of Scotland as a home for deaconesses, and in 1954 it was sold to Stirling Town Council for use as an old folk's home. With ten bedrooms on the first floor and three on the second floor, it was converted to accommodate 30 people. The large kitchen garden was planned to supply the home with fresh vegetables. Batterflats has since been sold and is now in the private sector again. The six acres are covered by a 1980s private housing development.

The testing and display of Stirling's new fire engine along Allan Park and Dumbarton Road, 6 April 1905. The horse-drawn engine was obtained at a cost of £265, a price which included the training of the brigade members. It was superceded by a motor-powered engine in 1923.

The funeral procession of Alexander McGregor, slater and fireman who was killed when accidentally thrown from a fire engine on a call. Photographed in October 1926, the procession is going up King Street to the cemetery at the Top of the Town.

As might be expected of a town taking all of the north-south traffic through Scotland, motoring accidents were numerous. In this road safety campaign, run by the Stirling and Clackmannan Police in 1959, the 28 deaths and 1,051 injuries of the previous year are highlighted on the roof rack of the Austin A55 'manumatic' saloon. Road deaths in Stirlingshire peaked at a figure of 53 for 1979, but since then there has been a steady reduction of fatalities. In the wider area covered by Central Scotland Police, and with greatly increased traffic on the roads, road deaths in 2006 and 2007 totalled eighteen for each year.

In 1928 the new Stirling Royal Infirmary was built on the estate of Easter Livilands on the south side of Stirling. It was designed by Glasgow architect and Stirling resident James Miller (1860–1947), and took the place of the old hospital in Spittal Street. Over the decades, the SRI has covered the estate to capacity. The structures in the foreground were built during the Second World War. The maternity unit was located at Airthrey Castle between 1941 and 1967. It moved back to a new two-storey purpose-built unit that year when the Airthrey Estate was acquired for the new University of Stirling. The chest diseases unit, built in 1955 was of major importance as Stirling was the hub of the Central Scotland mining industry, and the respiratory diseases which unfortunately came with it. Chest physician and Stirling Provost Dr Robert McIntyre was instrumental in securing the Airthrey Estate for the University. In 2006, plans were made to resite hospital facilities in Larbert and this new hospital is presently under construction.

Before the introduction of the NHS, a Charity Week was run in Stirling to raise funds for Stirling Royal Infirmary. Here, a troupe of 'foreigners' arrive at Stirling Station in 1939 with their leader, 'Akin Skinye', to meet J.J. Munro, Manager of the Regal Cinema, where their fund-raising 'Showtime' concert would take place.

A football signed by the members of the Scottish and English teams playing at Hampden Park, 17 April 1937. The ball was auctioned in aid of Stirling Royal Infirmary in May that year, during a fund-raising football match fought by Ministers and Doctors against the Police. The photograph was taken by Bannockburn photographer John G. Wilson.

St Ninians was a separate village on the south side of Stirling. *The Ordnance Gazetteer of Scotland* (1893) describes it as 'nominally one and a quarter miles south of Stirling [but] is in reality a straggling appendage to that town … It consists mainly of one long narrow street along the great south road from Stirling, just to the north of the point where it forks into the roads leading to Glasgow and Edinburgh. The houses are curious and old fashioned, and many of them bear rude sculpturings of dates, initials and sometimes the tools of the tradesmen to whom they originally belonged. St Ninians has a share in the woollen industries connected with Stirling, Bannockburn and Cambusbarron, and has besides a manufacture of nails and screwbolts of its own as well as tan works of a considerable size.'

Cambusbarron Main Street and the road to Touch, looking towards 'the West End'. The Foresters Arms, on the corner of Murray Place (locally known as 'the Coo Loan') was one of two public houses in the village. The building is still a public house today. The other pub, the Star Inn, at one time owned by the village blacksmith, was next door, but is not apparent in the photograph. These two public houses were the main places of entertainment in the village. Frequented by the workers from the nearby Hayford Mills, the pubs were especially busy with Irish navvies during the building of the North Third Reservoir (1906–1909) which is now one of the sources of Stirling's water supply.

The only road traffic here is the horse-drawn float with the beer kegs, and a pram on the other side. Note the one-legged man, who was probably a casualty of one of the wars of Empire. The date is *c.*1910.

The foot of The Brae, Cambusbarron. The building in the left foreground was a disused mill, acquired by the United Free Church of Scotland in 1860 and developed as a 'Mission Station'. In that year, Cambusbarron 'was the resort, especially on the Sabbath, of the idle and dissolute of the neighbouring town and villages, and became on these occasions a den of wickedness' (as quoted in *Bygone Days in Cambusbarron* (1981) by Peter Paterson). The parish church for the people of Cambusbarron was St Ninians, in the neighbouring village, and until the Bruce Memorial Church was built in 1910, the UF Mission was the only local place of worship. It later served as a garage, before being cleared away with much of the older housing on The Brae, in the 1970s.

Much of this part of St Ninians still survives and the houses in Kirk Wynd have been refurbished. The steeple was built for the mediaeval church in 1734. The church was used as a gunpowder store for the Jacobite army, which was besieging Stirling Castle in 1746. When news came of the imminent arrival of the Duke of Cumberland's army, the Jacobites retreated, fleeing across the Forth at the Fords of Frew as the south end of the Stirling Bridge had already been demolished to stop their passage. The villagers attempted to save some powder for themselves, and in the struggle with the Jacobites the church was blown up, killing nine villagers and three Highlanders. A new parish church was built nearby in the 1750s. The steeple was refurbished in 2006, and is still a landmark to those entering Stirling from the A872/A9 Glasgow Road today.

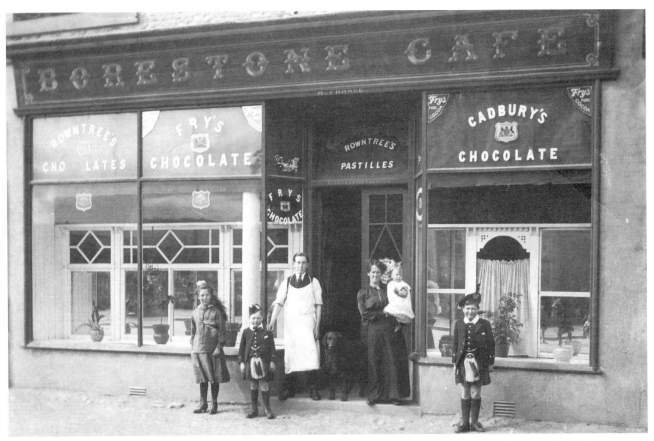

The Borestone Café, at 55 Borestone Crescent, St Ninians, was a haven for visitors travelling to see the Borestone on the field of Bannockburn. The café was run by Abe and Mary France, who also had a petrol filling station on the opposite side of the road.

The Borestone is traditionally the place where King Robert the Bruce planted his standard, prior to the Battle of Bannockburn. The site has been visited and venerated for generations. On 26 August 1787, Robert Burns came and 'said a fervent prayer for Old Caledonia over the hole of a blue whinstone where Robert the Bruce fixed his Royal standard on the banks of Bannockburn'. The Dumbarton Oddfellows raised the huge flagpole in 1870 to landmark the Borestone, and the little tin hut was added as a shelter for the guide. The land was secured for the National Trust for Scotland when it was threatened with building development in 1930. A commemorative cairn was added by the Guildry of Stirling in 1957, and in 1964 these features were encircled by a rotunda, commemorating the 650th anniversary of the battle.

The great equestrian statue of King Robert the Bruce, by Charles d'Orville Pilkington Jackson (1875–1973), was unveiled by the Queen at Bannockburn in 1964 to mark the 650th anniversary of the battle. Jackson was the foremost Scottish sculptor of his generation. Fund raising was difficult for the project and only secured when Canadian philanthropist, Eric Harvie QC, ordered a duplicate copy and paid for both. Bruce at Bannockburn has become one of the most photographed statues in Scotland. This picture by freelance press photographer A.D.S MacPherson emphasises the movement of horse and rider.

'Old Stirling is built on solid rock' is the title of this photograph by A.D.S. MacPherson. The excavation was for the extension to the Municipal Buildings in Corn Exchange in the early 1960s, and similar situations have been encountered all over the City of the Rock.

The National Wallace Monument which graces the skyline of Stirling to the north, was hewn out of the solid rock of the Abbey Craig. Designed by Glasgow architect J.T. Rochead and built between 1861 and 1869, it is seen here in the 1880s, reflected in the water of the quarry from which it came.

The employees of the North British Art Furniture Manufactory, 24 June 1887, prior to their taking part in the procession to the National Wallace Monument for the unveiling of the Wallace statue by D.W. Stevenson on the exterior of the building. It was a proud civic occasion, involving most of the public organisations in the burgh. Each man from this furniture works made a piece of model furniture and carried it on a pole for the appreciation of the crowds. Two of the models are now in the collection of the Stirling Smith. The factory in Forth Street was set up by architect J.W. Small, who wrote books on historic furniture and architecture. It closed down when he moved to South Africa in 1904, but vestiges of the furniture-making trade can be found in Stirling to this day.

The Abbey Craig Laundry at Causewayhead was a major employer of female labour for a generation. The works also undertook dry cleaning, carpet beating and carpet shampooing. This photograph was taken on 19 May 1932.

Now! Your Clothes Need A Holiday

They Need

Abbey Craig
Cleaning

IF YOU WANT
TO ENJOY
THEM NEXT
SEASON

Telephone 131

Near to the Abbey Craig Laundry at Causewayhead was the Grampian Motor and Engineering Works. Flight was pioneered through this company, by the Barnwell Brothers, in 1911. The works had a lucrative export market for their soil and other sterilisation machines. Steam sulphur generators were supplied to HM India Office for use in Rangoon. Grampian also built motor cars and cycles, steam tractors and boilers. The works closed in 2003.

Grampian Engineering workers, just before 1914, with three of the latest hospital sterilising machines. These were manufactured until the 1940s.

Until the collieries were closed in the wake of the miners' strike of 1984/85, Stirling was home to many of the miners of the Central Scotland coalfields. Coal was mined in the area from mediaeval times, but the sinking of modern collieries in the early 1900s saw a great influx of miners from other parts of Scotland and from Ireland. The poor working conditions in mines such as Cowie (opened 1896), Milhall (1904) and Fallin (1905), shown in this collage, was matched by the sub-standard housing provided by the colliery owners. The miners who did not manage to get housing in the eastern villages of Bannockburn, Plean, Cowie and Fallin crowded into the slums at the Top of the Town or, in the early twentieth century, got a bunk in the Miners' Hostel on Burghmuir.

Wallace Row in Cowie, *c*.1900. Typical of miners' housing, this was brick built and had few facilities for the residents.

The interior of a miner's house in the village of Standburn, east Stirlingshire, c.1910. The poor quality of the structure, lack of plumbing, adequate flooring and damp proofing were topics of public concern which ultimately led to the provision of municipal housing. When the Stirling Miners' Welfare Institute opened in the Craigs in March 1929, it had three baths to compensate for the lack of baths in local housing.

By the 1950s the council housing of 'New Cowie' had taken the place of the old rows. The white building in the centre is the Miners' Institute and the Fallin coal bing is on the left.

Cowie District and Polmaise Pipe Band, *c*.1920. The eastern villages had a strong community identity on account of the mining industry, and this found cultural expression in pipe, brass and silver bands, and in other events. For example, the Stirling Miners' Welfare Burns Supper in 1930 was the largest in the area with 400 attending.

'From the darkness into the light'. This painting by A.D.S. MacPherson, in the collections of the Stirling Smith, was made from his photograph, taken in the early 1960s of a young miner coming off the night shift into a bright summer morning. The photographer was so impressed with the strength and character of the miner that he painted the image in oils, the only medium he felt could do proper justice to the subject.

A view of the Airthrey Estate before the building for the University of Stirling began in 1966. In the decades since, the University has flourished, developing excellence in the subjects of education, nursing, history, sport and aquaculture. It runs Howietoun Fish Farm, established in 1873 and one of the first modern fish farms in the world, both as a commercial concern and as a research unit. The popularity and success of the University is rooted in its beautiful setting and in its reputation as one of the loveliest campuses in the world.

Established in 1967, the University of Stirling was the first to be built in Scotland after the mediaeval foundations of St Andrews, Aberdeen, Glasgow and Edinburgh. The privilege of having the new university was contested by Falkirk and Inverness, but the beauty and availability of the Airthrey Estate, between Stirling and Bridge of Allan, was one of the deciding factors. This view from 1968 shows Airthrey Loch and the Halls of Residence.

'Look around these historic surroundings. Under the Wallace Crag our national hero led his men against Cressingham. Within three miles, Bruce broke the chivalry of England at Bannockburn. Burns has wandered in those hills. In Stirling Castle our historic parliaments stayed for centuries, alternating with Edinburgh and Linlithgow. The eternal hills still look down on us as they looked down on Wallace and Bruce. The same snell wind coming up from the Western Isles still breathes on us today. The same sun pours its rays on us. The same mist fills the corries of the hills. The same spates fill our rivers. And I would fain, my friends, hope that the same spirit fills the heart of every Scotsman in his demand for a parliament in Edinburgh.'

These words were spoken by the novelist, poet and politician, Robert Bontine Cunninghame Graham at the foundation meeting of the National Party of Scotland, in the King's Park on 23 June 1928. Stirling has always been a landscape of inspiration, embedded in our literary and artistic heritage, and part and parcel of our national cultural heritage. It continues to inspire poets, politicians and artists to this day.

A view from the Wallace Monument, taken by A.D.S. MacPherson.